THE
Woodworker's
Visual Guide to Pricing
Your Work

KERRY PIERCE

POPULAR WOODWORKING BOOKS
CINCINNATI, OHIO
www.popularwoodworking.com

Other fine Popular Woodworking Books are available from your local bookstore or direct from the publisher.

Visit our Web site at www.popularwoodworking.com for information on more resources for woodworkers.

03 02 01 00 99   5 4 3 2 1

Library of Congress Cataloging-in-Publication Data

Pierce, Kerry.
  The woodworker's visual guide to pricing your work / by Kerry Pierce.—1st ed.
     p.   cm.
  Includes index.
  ISBN 1-55870-507-4 (alk. paper)
  1. Woodwork—Prices. 2. Home-based business. 3. Selling—Handicraft. I. Title.
TT200.P484   1999
684′.08′0688—dc21

99-21733
CIP

Edited by R. Adam Blake
Designed by Angela Lennert Wilcox
Production coordinated by John Peavler
Cover designed by David Mill

The profiles of Mark Arnold, Joe Graham and David Wright have previously appeared in *Woodwork* magazine.

METRIC CONVERSION CHART		
TO CONVERT	**TO**	**MULTIPLY BY**
Inches	Centimeters	2.54
Centimeters	Inches	0.4
Feet	Centimeters	30.5
Centimeters	Feet	0.03
Yards	Meters	0.9
Meters	Yards	1.1
Sq. Inches	Sq. Centimeters	6.45
Sq. Centimeters	Sq. Inches	0.16
Sq. Feet	Sq. Meters	0.09
Sq. Meters	Sq. Feet	10.8
Sq. Yards	Sq. Meters	0.8
Sq. Meters	Sq. Yards	1.2
Pounds	Kilograms	0.45
Kilograms	Pounds	2.2
Ounces	Grams	28.4
Grams	Ounces	0.04

Although my name is on the cover, it wouldn't be entirely accurate to say that I wrote this book. Most of the thinking was done by the men and women who agreed to share their woodwork and their experiences. In particular, I would like to thank Judy Ditmer, who took the time to compose several insightful essays which can be found within.

Thanks, too, for Elaine, Emily and Andy.

About the Author

Kerry Pierce has been a professional woodworker for more than 20 years and is the author of several woodworking books, including *Small-Production Woodworking for the Home Shop, Making Elegant Gifts From Wood* and *The Art of Chair Making.*

TABLE OF CONTENTS

The Work

PAGE 28

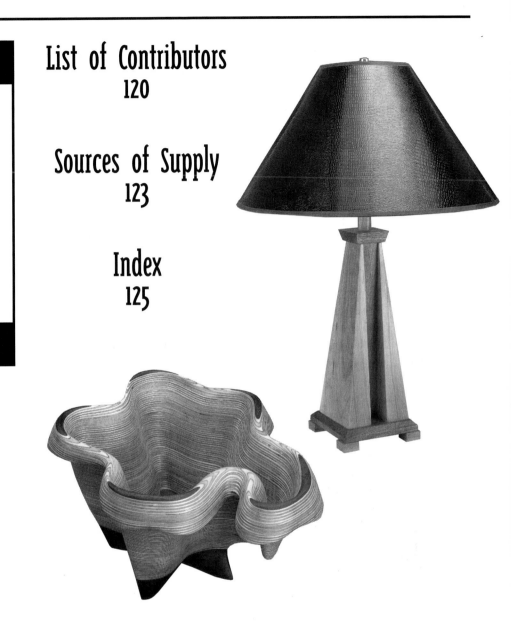

INTRODUCTION

There are as many different ways for woodworkers to set prices as there are woodworkers. Some individuals are meticulous about calculating the cost of labor, material and overhead, even adding on a percentage for profit. Others—particularly those whose reputations permit them to demand high prices—are often only marginally concerned about this kind of record keeping. They may set prices based solely on what they see as the quality of the individual work. Most fall somewhere in-between, making some effort to track the cost of labor and material but relying largely on intuition.

Many young and inexperienced woodworkers set prices based exclusively on labor and material. This fact may be related to their perceived need to justify their prices to their customers. ("This turned vessel is $150 because the materials cost $30 and it took me 12 hours to make.") Unfortunately, in their eagerness to make their prices comprehensible, these woodworkers often fail to account for the true cost of their work, neglecting to consider many hidden costs (overhead) of shop operation. They may pay themselves $15 or $20 an hour, but they don't compensate themselves for shop rental and up-keep, tool setup and maintenance, utilities, insurance, designing, estimating, sales and marketing—all of which are critical to the success of their woodworking operations.

More experienced woodworkers, particularly those whose work has been recognized as outstanding by the media and by their peers, often take a different view of pricing. ("These materials cost $40, and I worked maybe 18 hours, so I'll put on a price of $2,200.") True: The design and engineering processes may have percolated for days in some back corner of that woodworker's mind, but there is little connection between labor/material tracking and price, even after factoring in a cost for these invisible labors. Nevertheless, these woodworkers meet the financial needs of their businesses and families without consciously factoring overhead and profit into their prices.

Experience is not the only factor in setting prices. Lifestyle issues play a role. Some woodworkers feel their prices must be high enough to support a fairly luxurious standard of living. Several years ago, while interviewing woodworkers for my book *Small-Production Woodworking for the Home Shop*, I visited the home of a nationally known craftsman. Situated in the country, surrounded by hundreds of acres of lush green pasture, his large brick home looked more like the residence of a prominent industrialist than a prominent craftsman. Other woodworkers, however, have a different view. One of the chairmakers whose work appears in this book—Curtis Buchanan—says one of the keys to setting prices is being "satisfied with less junk." The merits of this idea are obvious. We would all do well to focus less on the material world.

Most in the woodworking field fall somewhere between these extremes. Most didn't go into the field to get rich, but they are, nevertheless, concerned about attaining a measure of economic security for themselves and their families.

One way to achieve that security is to develop solid price-setting strategies, which not only allow for the continued existence of the woodworker's business, but also permit that woodworker to live in a decent home, drive a decent car and send his or her children to college. In my opinion, these aren't unreasonable goals, even for someone who has chosen to make a living as a woodworker. It is my hope that this book will aid in establishing those price-setting strategies.

Sales
Methods

Any examination of the way woodwork is priced should include a look at the different methods by which it is sold, since each of these methods involves different, although related, pricing issues.

Commissions

The commission is the classic scenario for the sale of individually made furniture. The customer initiates this process by coming to the woodworker with a set of needs, which the woodworker attempts to refine by asking questions.

> " *Most woodworkers don't know how to sell. Too many consider it beneath their dignity as an artist/craftsman. This is a fatal attitude.*"
>
> **MIKE DUNBAR, HAMPTON, NH**

> " *The most satisfying part of my job is seeing the expressions on customers' faces when they see the finished project. For weeks this has only been a sketch on paper. Now they can reach out and touch their new furniture.*"
>
> **RANDY BEMONT, GRANBY, CT**

If, for example, the customer has come to the woodworker for a sideboard, the questions might focus on the dimensions of the sideboard, the arrangement of drawers and doors, the style of other dining room furniture with which it will be expected to coordinate, the materials and the finishes. Once the specifics of the design have been determined, the woodworker develops a material list and an approximation of the number of hours required by the construction of that sideboard. Then, after factoring in compensation for overhead and profit, the woodworker arrives at a price, which is then presented to the customer.

Ideally, there is no mention of a dollar amount until material, time, overhead and profit have been calculated. However, it often happens that the customer asks for a ballpark figure early in the design stage. Some woodworkers are reluctant to give this kind of estimate because they believe, quite rightly, they can't identify a price until they've figured the job. In some such cases, it's possible to deflect the customer's request, but at other times it's in the woodworker's best interest to provide the customer with this very rough estimate, since the customer may not realize whether an individually made sideboard is in the $800 range or in the $8,000 range. If the customer is thinking $800 and the woodworker is thinking $8,000, the simple act of offering this ballpark figure might save the woodworker a great deal of pointless design and calculation. Of course, many woodworkers address this problem in a different way: They charge a fee for figuring estimates. This fee then compensates them for the time and effort of producing a bid even if that bid is rejected.

In this classic scenario, the woodworker may feel he or she can stand firmly on the calculated price because, after all, the customer initiated the discussion. However, many factors can affect the firmness of that calculated price, some of them psychological.

If, for example, the woodworker is well established with a six-month backlog of work, the woodworker may categorically reject any attempt to reduce the price. If, however, the woodworker is relatively inexperienced and lacks that six-month backlog of work, he or she may want to back off just a bit if the client seems uncomfortable with the calculated price. This might be particularly true for someone who has just learned that they must replace the 5 hp motor on their table saw. However, lowering a bid for one customer can set a troublesome precedent: Other customers may then expect similar concessions.

Negotiating skill is another factor that can influence the firmness of the calculated price. Not all woodworkers are comfortable with the negotiating process, and a customer who is forceful and demanding can sometimes reduce a price through sheer force of will. Similarly, woodworkers who are very confident of their negotiating technique can sometimes persuade customers to spend more than they intend or can afford. Rarely, however, does a deal made under duress result in a successful woodworker/customer relationship.

Retail Shows

Many of the woodworkers whose work appears on these pages sell primarily through retail shows. This method can be very rewarding psychologically as well as financially because, like commission work, it puts the woodworker in direct contact with buyers, a contact that isn't possible with, for example, gallery or gift-shop sales. It can also be very humbling, particularly when the woodworker attempts a true accounting of the labor involved in even a single retail show.

Typically, the process begins many months before the show opens. In January, for example, a woodworker might begin the application procedure for a show he or she hopes to do in July or August. That procedure requires application forms, professionally taken slides of finished work, as well as an often-nonreturnable application fee. These materials must be prepared and sent off by a stipulated date so the slides can be reviewed by the show's jurors. Several months later, the woodworker is notified of acceptance or rejection. If accepted, the woodworker then submits the required booth fee. But whether accepted or not, the woodworker has invested both money and time in applying to that particular show.

Then work must be prepared. The goods displayed at a single weekend show in July might take all of February to create.

And the weekend of the show is even more work. Typically an exhibitor begins to set up at 7:00 or 8:00 A.M. for a show that opens at 9:00 A.M. The exhibitor then remains at the booth all day until the show closes at 9:00 P.M. Of course, the customers are rarely cleared from the facility until 10:00 P.M. or later, at which time the exhibitor must pack up to return to the motel and sleep a few hours before the next day begins.

The prices set on the objects sold at retail shows must account for the many nonproduction hours such a show requires, as well as the application, travel and lodging expenses incurred in connection with that show.

This is over and above the woodworker's normal overhead. In addition, sales at a retail show, like commission sales, should stipulate a profit.

Wholesale Shows

At a wholesale show, an exhibitor is less interested in selling specific objects from the booth than in establishing a relationship with buyers that may last many years. If, for example, a representative from a chain of gift shops sees an appealing humidor at one of the show's booths, that representative might order ten humidors a month from the exhibitor who made them. Several such accounts can relieve some of the financial pressure from a woodworker's operation. However, there is a cost for this relief.

First, wholesale shows typically charge higher booth fees than retail shows, and second, buyers expect to purchase goods at a much lower price than the woodworker would charge for those same goods at a retail show. This lower price permits the wholesale buyer to add a respectable markup without alienating that buyer's potential retail customers. Because of the buyer's expectation of a lower price, a woodworker must be very careful about selling at wholesale shows. An order for 100 humidors is worse than useless if the woodworker is only making $3 or $4 an hour to build those humidors.

When considering wholesale shows, the woodworker must balance the rewards of a guaranteed income against the very real expenses of operating a shop. In fact, some woodworkers find that wholesale shows are simply unworkable because, in their view, the product they make can't be offered at a low enough price to attract a wholesale buyer.

> " As a small business—a one-man band—the greatest challenge I face is booking enough work to earn a living but not too much so as to deliver orders late."
>
> **CHRIS KAMM, ARDEN, NC**

> " The most difficult aspect of making a living as a woodworker has to be finding a market for your product. With so many discount furniture shops selling junk, you have to educate your customers about furniture quality. This then relates to your final price."
>
> **RANDY BEMONT, GRANBY, CT**

The Value of a Reputation

Several years ago, I interviewed Brian Boggs, the nationally known chair-maker from Berea, Kentucky, for an article in Woodwork *magazine. As he looked back over his career, he made this comment: "Fourteen years ago, if I had made these same chairs [referring to the chairs then being produced in his shop], I couldn't have sold them, not for the prices I'm now charging. And it wouldn't have been because inflation* is *the difference.*

"When someone walks in and sees a chair they like, they still don't know if it's good. They only know that it looks good and feels good, and it's comfortable. They don't know if the chair is *good.*

"The only thing that tells them whether or not that chair is going to be with them through the next generation is the sense they get from the craftsman about the chair's integrity. They have to believe what I'm telling them. They have to believe me when I tell them that joint was fully dry when I put it together. They also have to get a sense, when they look at the chair, that this piece is made right. And you're not going to be able to convince anybody of that when you're starting out."

Q: **How would you best describe the way your work reaches the public?**

A: 57% said "Word of mouth."
53% said "Retail shows."
23% said "Print ads."
13% said "Wholesale shows."
10% said "Own catalog."
3% said "Web site."

Note: The percentages total over 100% because many respondents identified more than one method.

Galleries

From the perspective of the woodworker, there are two kinds of galleries: one good and one bad.

Some galleries make outright purchase of the artist's work for later resale. These are the good galleries.

The consignment gallery is the other kind, and they operate a little differently. The owner of the consignment gallery agrees to display the work in return for a large cut of the selling price, often as high as 50 percent. From the perspective of the woodworker, these are the bad galleries because the woodworker is paid nothing unless and until the work is sold by the gallery.

Although consignment galleries may be good places to offer large, speculative pieces, prices must take into account the extremely unpredictable nature of gallery sales. The prices must be small enough to accommodate the often 100 percent markup, but they must still be large enough to compensate the woodworker for labor, material and overhead, in addition to profit. To some woodworkers, this means that gallery prices should be very high. (Why speculate when the possible returns are small?) On the other hand, some woodworkers see galleries as outlets for pieces they really wanted to make even though no client had ordered them: pieces the woodworker would feel content to sell at a lower price, one that may compensate them for no more than labor and material.

Catalogs

Today it's possible for a woodworker with a computer, a scanner, a high-quality printer and a smattering of knowledge to put together a professional-looking catalog. Although technology has simplified the process of creating a catalog, selling through that catalog is not without its share of complications.

When pricing items for catalog sales, consider the lifespan of those prices. While prices at a retail booth can be adjusted from show to show (or even from moment to moment at the same show), catalog prices must be set so those prices will remain in the woodworker's comfort zone a month or six months down the road. If that is not the case, make a prominent notation in the catalog identifying the term of the published prices. Another, perhaps better, solution to this problem is the removable price sheet. Ed and Carole Schmidt, toy makers from Reynoldsburg, Ohio, do very well offering their line of well-made, solid-wood toys through a 16-page catalog. But the prices aren't printed on the pages of the catalog. They are, instead, printed on a photocopied sheet tipped into each catalog. This way they can update prices without reprinting the entire catalog.

Internet

Woodworkers, being perhaps gadget happy by nature, seem to have taken quite naturally to the Internet, and woodworking Internet sites are proliferating like buttonweed in a bean field. It remains to be seen, however, how successful this type of marketing will be in the long run. It's hard to imagine, for example, a client buying a $10,000 carved carousel horse based solely on a grainy Internet image, although there are dozens of these horses offered there. It seems more likely that the Internet will be a medium through which a woodworker can establish a first contact with a customer, a contact that might later turn into a sale or into a group of sales.

Setting Prices

Setting prices is not a process that can be examined in isolation. It must be viewed in the context of the woodworker's life, work and goals. For example, the individual who wants to pick up a few dollars at local weekend retail shows will approach the process in a much different way than the individual whose shop is his or her only source of income. Also, the prices set by the woodworking professional with 25 years of experience and a national reputation are apt to be quite different than those set by the beginning professional who just quit his day job.

The only constants are labor, material, overhead and profit; and these issues, too, are often difficult to examine in isolation. If a turner buys a 50-yard roll of abrasives and then uses that roll in the creation of six different vases, each of which requires a different amount of sanding, to which job is the cost of that roll charged? If a maker of casework is interrupted by a 20-minute phone conversation from a potential new customer, is the time spent on that call charged to the interrupted job or to the potential new job, which may or may not ever materialize? Overhead is a particularly unpredictable element in this financial equation. If, after years of sanding panels with hand-held machines, the woodworker buys a 36″-wide belt sander, a year's worth of overhead will come crashing down on the shop's budget in an instant. Profit, too, can be difficult to calculate in isolation. Judy Ditmer, a turner from Dayton, Ohio, makes the point that although she rarely sells large bowls at retail shows, the presence of those bowls in her portfolio often enhances her prospects of getting past the shows' juries. It may be impossible, then, to attribute any profit to the bowls being

shown at a particular show, but that fact doesn't diminish the importance of those bowls to the possibility of making profit from other sales at that show.

There are also psychological factors that affect the process of setting prices. When I first began work on this book, a friend offered the observation that ego might be a critical element in this process, that the prices marked on an individual's work might be seen by the customer and by the woodworker as, in some way, a reflection of the woodworker's worth, and this is an opinion I have often heard expressed by people in the woodworking community. A maker of small boxes once told me he didn't want to set his prices too low because some retail show customers see the maker of $25 boxes as less of a craftsman than the individual whose boxes start at $100. Similarly, some purchasers of commission work—particularly those who like to make statements with their wallets—seek out the craftsman with the highest prices, believing that expensive work carries with it more status and more value. Recognizing this, woodworkers, too, may believe there is a connection between their worth and the prices their work can command. This situation is particularly troublesome for younger and less established woodworkers. While they may be talented and accomplished, the absence of a recognizable name can prevent them from getting the kind of prices their work would otherwise merit. I think Beth Ann Harrington, who makes beautiful Mission-style case work in her shop in Medford, Massachusetts, puts it most plainly: "Pricing my work is very difficult. Because the work is so personal—I made it—and I'm trying to put a value on my skills, it's hard not to get

emotionally involved and to feel vulnerable and insecure."

The process can be daunting, but it's not hopeless. In fact, in a production shop, it's possible to do a very accurate analysis of item cost. In a shop that makes coat racks in lots of 100 or 500, the time and material for a run of 100 can be totaled and divided by 100 to yield a per-item cost very close to the item's true labor-and-material cost. However, not all woodworkers think in terms of 100-item lots.

How then can cost be calculated?

The answer is that, in most shops, it can't be calculated with absolute

> *The most difficult aspect of woodworking as a career is explaining to an uneducated public why I demand the prices I do. Too many people have bought into the myth of Ethan Allen and other High Point, North Carolina, furniture companies. Often, I feel like I'm fighting a losing battle when I explain the construction and finish of a piece to a prospective client who declines my bid saying, 'I'm not looking to spend that much,' then drives off in a new Lexus.*
>
> *"In a world where appearance is everything, few people are willing to spend a little extra to get a really well-made piece of furniture. If the end result looks the same, who cares how it's made or what it is made of?"*
>
> **MARK ARNOLD, POWELL, OH**

precision. The woodworker must begin by accepting the fact that he or she may never know whether that Shaker document chest takes 8.9 hours to build or 9.8, whether that Brewster chair requires $6 worth of abrasives or $16, whether that entertainment center earns a $250 profit or a $300 profit. It is possible, however, to generate useful information through the study of any shop's operations.

In this regard, accurate record keeping is essential.

The notion of keeping accurate records might make some woodworkers squirm. After all, no one becomes a woodworker to do paperwork, but establishing prices that are fair to the woodworker, as well as to the cus-

> " Since mine is a small custom-furniture shop (two employees), prices are determined by adding materials to estimated hours times shop rate. My shop rate is a combination of overhead plus a modest profit (15 percent). Since I use labor-intensive methods—i.e., mortise-and-tenon instead of biscuits, etc.—I cannot and do not try to compete with retail furniture outlets. They have an economy of scale that can't be touched when I produce only one-of-a-kind pieces."
>
> **MARK ARNOLD, POWELL, OH**

tomer, requires a clear understanding of the true cost of the objects being sold. Without record keeping, that understanding is impossible to achieve. Fortunately, the process is not as intimidating as it might at first seem, particularly for work done on speculation.

Material costs are easily tracked. Receipts can be slipped into a folder labeled with the job name, then totaled when the job is complete. Labor records are nearly as simple to maintain. Hours and fractions of hours devoted to a particular job can be noted on a clipboard hung near the shop door or above the shop desk. True, leftover materials from one job may be used later for another job, and the time records are sometimes estimations, but this data, although imperfect, can still be useful.

The amount of overhead is a bit more difficult to track, but once again, accurate record keeping is the key. A woodworker can begin by taking the time to list the various "hidden costs" of shop operation. The items on that sheet might include shop utilities, shop maintenance, tool purchase and maintenance, insurance on the premises, as well as liability insurance should an accident occur in a customer's home while the woodworker is delivering or installing work. It might also include such items as health insurance and retirement, since many traditional employers provide these for their workers.

The specific list of inclusions must be determined by each individual woodworker after an examination of that woodworker's personal and professional circumstances. For example, a woodworker whose spouse receives employer-provided family health coverage won't need to consider the cost of health insurance when calculating the amount of overhead, and the

woodworker who rents rather than owns a shop must remember to include shop rent in his or her calculation.

These expenses can be tracked over a period of time—two months, six months, a year. They can then be charged against the work produced during that period of time. For instance, if the overhead costs for a two-month period totaled $800 and if six weeks of that period were spent in the construction of a set of twelve Shaker-style side chairs, $600 of "hidden costs" should be charged to those side chairs, adding $50 to the cost of each chair. The woodworker might then add that charge—$100 per week of shop operation—to all future sales.

Of course, not all "hidden costs" are equal. Some are one-time expenses—a computer purchase, for example—that can be prorated over a finite period. Others, like phone service, are monthly charges that will continue as long as the business exists. Still others might be described as emergency expenses. A nearly completed entertainment center that falls from a bench and is substantially ruined can be a crushing addition to any shop's overhead.

As accurately as possible, the woodworker should estimate the "hidden costs" involved in keeping the shop's doors open and then add that prorated cost to every item produced in that shop.

Then finally, there is the issue of profit. A business should make money over and above expenses. The amount of profit required or expected by a particular business can only be determined by the owner of that business, but if a business is to flourish, somewhere in the pricing equation there must be an allowance for profit.

Labor Record

For the shop of: _____

For the job: _____

> Usually, I pretty much know what my selling price needs to be. If it seems a little higher than comparable work others are selling, there are two possibilities:
>
> "One: the comparable work isn't really comparable, i.e., perhaps mine is superior in some fashion that makes it worth the extra cost to my customers. If my item is selling well, my assumption is that this is the case.
>
> "Two: my production of the item is somehow inefficient or I'm paying too much for the materials. If I believe this to be the case, and I still wish to make the item, I will attempt to address these issues.
>
> "Of course, there is also a third possibility: the other person has under-priced her work. Alas, this is too often true. Regardless of the reasons, this obviously affects my ability to sell similar work at the same venue. I may change the work or discontinue selling that item (at least at that venue), but I won't lower my price."
>
> **JUDY DITMER, PIQUA, OH**

Q: **How would you best describe the method by which you establish prices for your work?**

A: 53% of the contributors said "Educated guesses."
47% said "Totaling materials and labor costs."
23% said "Comparisons to prices charged by competitors."

Note: The percentages total over 100% because several respondents identified more than one method.

Commissioned Work

For the shop that focuses on custom one-of-a-kind work, the best way to figure the next job is to look at the last job. When a customer asks for a bid, the woodworker should look at the records for previously made pieces built on a similar scale.

If, for example, a customer wants a bid on a veneered sofa table, the woodworker might pull out the records for a previously constructed veneered table of approximately the same size and complexity. There, on those sheets, the woodworker can find an accounting of material and labor. By substituting in appropriate numbers for differences in material and by adding on the labor cost for the earlier table, as well as an overhead allowance and a profit percentage, the woodworker can produce a useful bid for the new customer's veneered sofa table.

Jonathan McLean, the creator of the magnificent bombe desk on page 53, explains that if someone were to order another copy of that desk, the first step in the bidding process would be consulting his records. "I have notes from when I made that piece, kind of like time cards I kept, and I could get a good idea of how long it would take to make a new one." Since the original was made in 1991, it would be necessary to plug into his labor estimate new hourly rates, but once that is done, he could produce a reasonably accurate estimate of labor costs for the new desk. After figuring current material costs, adding on an overhead allowance and a percentage for profit, he would have an accurate bid for the new edition of that desk.

Speculative Work

Speculative work—work done for galleries, for retail and wholesale shows, for any noncommissioned outlets—often involves a different set of price-setting strategies.

To this point, I've focused on what specialists in small business refer to as *cost pricing*, the calculated cost in terms of labor, material, overhead and profit. A second type of price particularly relevant to the creation of speculative work is *market-value pricing*. This term refers to the amount that the market will bear, which almost always varies from the *cost price* of a given item.

In this regard, John Pollock, a maker of band-sawn puzzle boxes in Toledo, Ohio, once told me about a young woodworker who visited John's shop for advice. John said the young man was an excellent craftsman with some appealing ideas for products, but John had to explain to the young man that "he couldn't make them [the products] for the price he would have to put on them to expect any sales." The *market-value price* would have been much lower than the *cost price*, making those items—at least in John's opinion—unsellable. This is the difficult lesson that *market-value pricing* teaches. Sometimes we can't get enough out of an object to make it worthwhile to produce that object.

In many cases, the market-value price for an object can be established by averaging the prices for other, similar objects produced by other woodworkers. However, when pricing a newly designed object significantly unlike anything offered by other woodworkers, the woodworker must make a decision about the item's *market-value price* guided only by intuition.

Unfortunately for the novice woodworker, in the matter of intuition, experience is the best possible guide. Richard Rothbard, a maker of band-sawn boxes from Slate Hill,

New York, explains how he sets the prices on his speculative pieces: "After my time studies, I look at the finished piece and ask if I can get the price derived or not. I then usually bump the price up based on what I consider the 'right' price for it to sell rather quickly." True: He does time study his work, but it's also true that his intuition about the *market-value price* of an object is the critical component in the establishment of his price.

The beginner who builds speculative pieces is likely to make significant pricing errors, listing some objects at such high prices that sales are inhibited, while listing others at such low prices that profit is nonexistent. These errors must be studied and addressed in later pricings, but to a certain extent, they must also be accepted as an inevitable part of acquiring experience.

Formula for Determining Cost Prices

Cost prices are relatively easy to calculate. The woodworker totals the cost of materials, adds to that a labor figure, which is the number of hours worked times that woodworker's hourly rate, then adds in an overhead charge appropriate for the number of hours worked, all of which is multiplied by a specified percentage for profit. The formula can be expressed this way:

(Cost of materials + (hours worked × hourly rate) + (hours worked × overhead rate)) × (1 + profit percentage) = cost price.

If, for example, a woodworker is selling bookshelves, each of which requires $28 in materials and 8 hours of labor, the calculation might look like this:

$28 in materials + 8 hours at $20

Materials

For the shop of: _____

For the job: _____

	Description	Cost
Primary wood:	_____	_____
Secondary wood:	_____	_____
Special tooling:	_____	_____
Hardware:	_____	_____
Finishing supplies: . . .	_____	_____
Abrasives:	_____	_____
Other materials:	_____	_____
	_____	_____
	_____	_____
	_____	_____
	_____	_____
	_____	_____
	_____	_____
	_____	_____
	_____	_____
	Total	_____

per hour labor + 8 hours at $1 per hour overhead, all multiplied by 1.20 (this allows for a 20% profit) = $235.20.

Formula for Determining Market-Value Prices

Market-value prices are even easier to calculate since they are nothing more than averages of prices charged by the competition. They do, however, require some legwork. If the woodworker making the shelves described above wants to develop an accurate sense of the market-value price of those shelves, that woodworker must check the prices of similar shelving units at retail shows, at galleries and in the catalogs of other woodworkers.

Once those prices have been identified, they are averaged. The formula can be expressed this way:

Total of prices divided by the number of units = market-value price.

If, for example, the woodworker has identified comparable shelving units selling for $225, for $221 and for $190, the calculation might look like this:

$225 + $221 + $190 divided by 3 = $212.

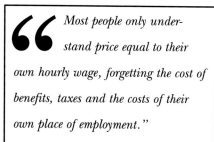

Most people only understand price equal to their own hourly wage, forgetting the cost of benefits, taxes and the costs of their own place of employment.

SAL CRETELLA, BRISTOL, CT

Bringing Cost Prices and Market-Value Prices Into Alignment

In a perfect world, cost prices would always be lower than market-value prices. Then, in that perfect world, the woodworker would simply raise his cost price up so that it agreed with the market-value price. However, in the real world in which we all actually live, it rarely works out that way. More typically, the cost price is higher than the market-value price and the woodworker is left then to decide how much of the cost price to give away in order to make that item's price competitive.

In the case of the woodworker making the previously discussed shelving units, the cost price is $23.20 more than the market-value price. Such a small difference (it represents under 10 percent of the cost price) is probably insignificant, so the woodworker may choose to maintain that cost price. However, in many cases, the cost price is significantly higher than the market-value price. In such a situation, the woodworker has a more troublesome decision to make: Should the product be abandoned or should the woodworker cut the price enough to make the shelving unit competitive?

Once again, experience is the best guide.

Raising Prices

As the cost of living rises, so too should the prices that woodworkers charge for their goods. Unfortunately, there are no guidelines stipulating exactly how this process should unfold. Some woodworkers, particularly those doing commission work in a low- or middle-income setting, may

find their customers will tolerate only the most modest of price increases. On the other hand, those woodworkers catering to an upscale customer base may find that even extravagant price increases are easily achieved.

Even in those upscale settings, price increases are most easily achieved when accompanied by the perception of increased value. In order to charge more money, the woodworker must convince potential customers that his work is worth more money. To a certain extent, this can be achieved by creating ever-better work. But often customers are not attuned to woodworking's nuances. They may not be able to see the differences between a Windsor settee with a $1,200 price tag and a similar but superior settee with a $2,500 price tag. However, if the craftsman's work has won a number of awards, if that work has been featured in magazines and newspapers, potential customers often have more confidence their purchase will provide years of satisfactory service as well as appreciate in value with the passage of time. This perception of increased value can translate into very real dollars at the time of the sale. In this regard, it's important for the craftsman to inform potential customers of any recognition their work might have received.

It's also possible to increase income without actually raising prices. I once asked Patrick Leonard, a maker of small case goods from Washington, Pennsylvania, about the process of raising prices. He explained that one of the ways he approaches this process is by streamlining his production techniques to make them more efficient so he can produce more work in less time, in that manner increasing income.

Overhead Calculation

For the shop of: _____

Per month

Shop rental or mortgage payment: . . . . _____

Shop maintenance: . . . . _____

Vehicle payment: . . . . _____

Vehicle maintenance: . . . . _____

Tool purchase: . . . . _____

Tool maintenance: . . . . _____

Electricity: . . . . _____

Phone: . . . . _____

Internet service: . . . . _____

Gas: . . . . _____

Water: . . . . _____

Insurance on building: . . . . _____

Medical insurance: . . . . _____

Vehicle insurance: . . . . _____

Other: . . . . _____

Monthly total: . . . . _____

Monthly total divided by 4 to yield per week total: _____ $\div$ 4 _____

Weekly total divided by 40 to yield per hour total: _____ $\div$ 40 _____

Pricing a Shaker-Style Carrier

This delicate carrier, patterned after one appearing in June Sprigg and Jim Johnson's book *Shaker Woodenware: A Field Guide,* lends itself to relatively quick production, particularly if done in lots of ten or more. The following discussion focuses on the establishment of a price for carriers made in such lots.

Overhead Calculation

The pricing strategy for a specific item must take into consideration the specific circumstances of the individual woodworker's overhead. The following conditions apply to objects produced in my shop.

- Shop rental: $0. (I own my own shop.)
- Shop maintenance: I estimate this to be less than $20 per month of full-time operation. (This amount includes biannual renewal of the roof coating as well as periodic painting of the building's trim. In both cases, I furnish the labor.)
- Vehicle purchase: $0. (I own the vehicle I use to pick up materials and deliver furniture.)
- Vehicle maintenance: $40 per month.
- Tool purchase: I estimate this to be less than $10 per month. (With rare exceptions—large, infrequently purchased machinery, for example—I include the cost of new tooling in the materials charges for the job that requires that new tool.)
- Tool maintenance: I estimate this to be less than $20 per month of full-time operation. (This figure includes sharpening services, as well as replacement parts for machinery.)
- Utilities: I estimate this to be $30 per month of full-time operation. (This includes electricity and the cost of operating the chainsaw necessary to keep my woodburner supplied with fuel throughout the winter.)
- Insurance on the building: I carry no special coverage on my shop. The shop's prorated portion of my homeowner's policy is less than $10 per month.
- Medical insurance and retirement: $0. (This is paid through the school for which I work.)

This gives me a total of $130 per month in overhead expenses required to keep my shop going through four weeks of full-time operation. That amount can then be apportioned at a rate of $32.50 per week (or $6.50 per day or $.81 per hour).

Note: As a part-time woodworker with an inclination to low-cost and low-tech tooling, my shop's operating costs are substantially lower than the operating costs of a full-time woodworker who uses high-tech and high-cost machinery.

These overhead calculations make no allowances for designing and marketing. Since this piece is a reproduction, no designing time was required. Since the piece was presold, no marketing expenses were incurred. Other woodworkers in other settings may need to include allowances for both designing and marketing.

Labor Calculation

If made in lots of ten or more, the per-unit construction time for this carrier is under 2 hours, even with hand-cut dovetails. At $15 per hour, the labor cost for this carrier is $30.

Overhead Calculation (for Carrier)

Since the overhead price in my shop has been identified as $.81 per hour, the overhead cost for this carrier is $1.62.

Material Calculation

Although there is less than a board foot of material in the finished carrier, I use almost three times that amount in its construction. This surplus allows me to cut around the defects in the low-grade material I use when constructing something with such small dimensions. At a bit less than $1 a foot, the material cost for each carrier is $3.

Profit Percentage

I allow a 20 percent profit percentage.

Final Calculation of Cost Price

Formula: (Cost of materials + (hours worked × hourly rate) + (hours worked × overhead rate)) × (1 + profit percentage) = cost price.

$3 in materials + 2 hours at $15 per hour labor + 2 hours at $.81 per hour overhead, all multiplied by 1.20 (this allows for a 20 percent profit) = $41.54 price per carrier.

Bringing Cost Price and Market-Value Price Into Alignment

Once the cost price is established, I look at the prices other woodworkers charge for similar objects. Although I don't find any carriers exactly like the one I've made, I do see enough similar objects to convince me that the cost price of $41.54 is a bit on the low side. In other words, the market-value price of this carrier is greater than the cost price.

I then decide to set a final price of $55 on the carrier.

Artist Kerry Pierce
Type of object carrier
Approximate size in inches $8 \times 5 \times 4$
Material cherry, ash, copper tacks
Estimated cost of material $3
Estimated hours of labor 2
Price $55
Photographer Kerry Pierce

Q: **Do you periodically adjust prices to reflect changing materials and labor costs?**

A: 76% of the contributors said ''Yes.''

Q: **Do you lower the price of an item that isn't selling?**

A: 70% of the contributors said ''No.''

Pricing a Stool With a Sculpted Seat

This sassafras and walnut stool (right) has a seat shaped by hand primarily through the use of a drawknife, an inshave and several spokeshaves. Because of the amount of hand work, the cost price of this stool is relatively high.

Labor Calculation

This stool has three turned legs and a hand-tool-shaped seat, requiring almost 8 hours of labor. At $15 per hour, the labor cost for this stool is $120.

Overhead Calculation

Using the method identified in the previous section, the overhead price in my shop is identified as $.81 per hour. At that rate, the 8 hours of labor require an overhead charge of $6.48.

Material Calculation

The sassafras seat requires almost two board feet of material, the walnut legs an additional two board feet.

Sassafras—when it's available—runs about $2 a foot. Walnut is never less than $4 a foot. This brings the material cost to $12.

Profit Percentage

I allow a 20 percent profit percentage.

Final Calculation of Cost Price

Formula: (Cost of materials + (hours worked × hourly rate) + (hours worked × overhead rate)) × (1 + profit percentage) = cost price.

$12 in materials + 8 hours at $15 per hour labor + 8 hours at $.81 per hour overhead, all multiplied by 1.20 (this allows for a 20 percent profit) = $166.18 price per stool.

Bringing Cost Prices and Market-Value Prices Into Alignment

Unlike the Shaker-style carrier, which seemed, by comparison to other similar objects, to be worth more than the amount of its cost price, this stool, by comparison to other similar objects, seems to be worth a bit less than its cost price. In other words, the market-value price of this stool is less than its cost price.

Because of that, I put a price of $120 on the stool.

> " *Pricing my work is very difficult. Because the work is so personal—I made it—and I'm trying to put a value on my skills, it's hard not to get emotionally involved and to feel vulnerable and insecure.*"
>
> BETH ANN HARRINGTON, MEDFORD, MA

Q: **Do you periodically adjust your prices to bring them in line with your competitor's prices?**

A: 86% of the contributors said "No."

Artist Kerry Pierce
Type of object stool
Approximate size in inches $8 \times 13 \times 19$
Material walnut, sassafras
Estimated cost of material $12
Estimated hours of labor 8
Price $120
Photographer Kerry Pierce

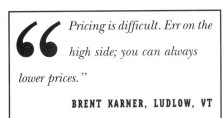

" *Pricing is difficult. Err on the high side; you can always lower prices.* "

BRENT KARNER, LUDLOW, VT

The Work

When does a jewelry box become a chest of drawers? Should functional wooden spoons be grouped with spoon-like sculptures? How about carved wooden bowls? Should they be grouped with turned wooden bowls? And when does a table become a desk?

I struggled for several weeks to group the photos into useful catego-ries, trying one combination after an-other. None seemed to work just right. The seating furniture section was particularly troublesome, con-taining side chairs, armchairs, rock-ing chairs, stools, settles, benches, etc. No matter how I divided that group, I failed to come up with mean-ingful categories.

Should a carved Chippendale side chair be grouped with a side chair having shaved posts and a hickory bark seat? What about Sal Cretella's attractive and informal benches? Did they belong in the same group as B.A. Harrington's much more formal oak settle?

I hope you find the following group-ings useful. I did the best I could.

BOXES

Artist Jim Fiola
Type of object box
Approximate size in inches $11 \times 22 \times 5\frac{3}{4}$
Material bird's-eye maple, padauk
Estimated cost of material $25
Estimated hours of labor 12 +
Price $495
Photographer Tom Hodge

> " *After designing, the most difficult aspect of making a living as a woodworker is making the product affordable so it can be sold. The good design is useless unless it can be purchased and used by the customer.*"
>
> **JIM FIOLA, BRANCHVILLE, NJ**

Q: **How would you best describe your woodworking training?**

A: 77% of the contributors said "Self-taught."
27% said "Apprenticeship."
27% said "Four-year college."
27% said "Two-year college."
10% said "High-school level vocational school."

Note: The percentages total over 100% because many respondents identified more than one.

Artist Jim Fiola

Type of object jewelry chest

Approximate size in inches $14 \times 14 \times 5\frac{1}{2}$

Material bird's-eye maple, wenge

Estimated cost of material $25

Estimated hours of labor 12+

Price $495

Photographer Tom Hodge

Artist Jim Fiola

Type of object jewelry chest

Approximate size in inches $14 \times 18 \times 9$

Material bird's-eye maple, wenge

Estimated cost of material $35

Estimated hours of labor 15+

Price $625

Photographer Tom Hodge

Artist Jim Fiola
Type of object
 humidor
Approximate size in
 inches $11 \times 14 \times 8\frac{1}{2}$
Material bubinga,
 cherry
Estimated cost of
 material $25 ($20
 for hygrometer
 and moisturizer)
Estimated hours of
 labor 9 +
Price $425
Photographer Tom
 Hodge

Artist Po Shun Leong
Type of object wall box
Approximate size in inches $36 \times 12 \times 7$
Material narra, mahogany, wenge, maple
Estimated cost of material $100
Estimated hours of labor 24
Price $4,500
Photographer Po Shun Leong

Artist Barry Middleton

Type of object jewelry box

Approximate size in inches $3 \times 12 \times 6$

Material bird's-eye maple, Australian lacewood

Estimated cost of material $15

Estimated hours of labor 2½

Price $200

Photographer Bob Barrett

Artist Barry Middleton

Type of object jewelry box

Approximate size in inches $3 \times 14 \times 6$

Material South American lacewood

Estimated cost of material $20

Estimated hours of labor 3

Price $375

Photographer David Egan

Artist Kerry Pierce
Type of object chest
Approximate size in inches
 $11\frac{5}{8} \times 18\frac{7}{8} \times 11\frac{3}{8}$
Material curly maple, pine
Estimated cost of material $65
Estimated hours of labor 15
Price $350
Photographer Adam Blake

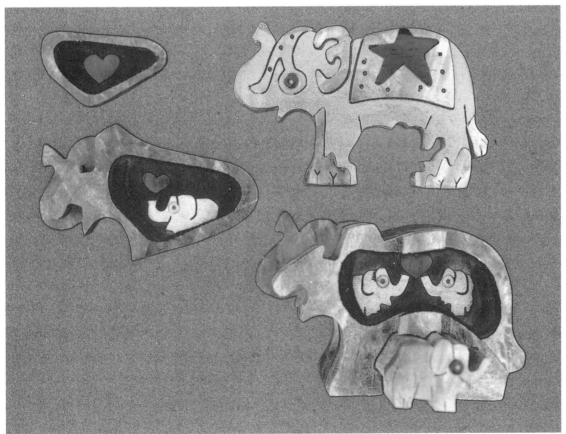

Artist Richard Rothbard
Type of object puzzle box
Approximate size in inches $1\frac{3}{4} \times 3 \times 1\frac{3}{4}$
Material poplar, redwood, maple, padauk
Estimated cost of material $2
Estimated hours of labor 4
Price $189
Photographer Maja

Artist Richard
Rothbard
Type of object puzzle
box
**Approximate size in
inches** 26×6×15
Material big leaf
maple burl
**Estimated cost of
material** $60
**Estimated hours of
labor** 12
Price $3,000
Photographer Manny
Gonzales

Artist Richard
Rothbard
Type of object box
**Approximate size in
inches** 8×8×3
Material California
buckeye,
bubinga, maple,
maple burl
**Estimated cost of
material** $35
**Estimated hours of
labor** 30
Price $1,800
Photographer Maja

Artist Kerry Pierce
Type of object wall box
Approximate size in inches
  $12\frac{1}{2} \times 12\frac{7}{8} \times 6\frac{5}{8}$
Material maple
Estimated cost of material $5
Estimated hours of labor 6
Price $150
Photographer Adam Blake

Artist Kerry Pierce
Type of object chest
Approximate size in inches
  $8\frac{5}{8} \times 15\frac{7}{16} \times 5\frac{9}{16}$
Material curly maple, walnut
Estimated cost of material $10
Estimated hours of labor 12
Price $250
Photographer Adam Blake

Artist Kerry Pierce

Type of object box

Approximate size in inches
13¾ × 12¾ × 9½

Material walnut, ash

Estimated cost of material $8

Estimated hours of labor 6

Price $150

Photographer Adam Blake

Artist Gregory K. Williams

Type of object jewelry chest

Approximate size in inches
9½ × 14½ × 8½

Material cherry, walnut

Estimated cost of material $30

Estimated hours of labor 10

Price $400

Photographer Terry Nelson

Artist Gregory K. Williams
Type of object jewelry chest
Approximate size in inches $9 \times 16 \times 10$
Material maple, walnut
Estimated cost of material $45
Estimated hours of labor 20
Price $450
Photographer Jerry Anthony

> " *Pricing is a reflection of my belief in the strength of my work. The best pieces are priced highest. Time and materials are considerations but far less than artistic or creative success.* "
>
> **NORM SARTORIUS, PARKERSBURG, WV**

MARK ARNOLD: REVISITING THE GOLDEN AGE OF AMERICAN FURNITURE

Mark Arnold, the owner of the Boston Woodworking Company in Powell, Ohio, speaks slowly and precisely, weighing each word before committing it to speech. His sentences unfold at a leisurely pace, one idea following another in a progression that is both unhurried and logical.

We sit at a small conference table in the office area of his shop's showroom, my tape recorder between us. Albert Sack's book, *The Fine Points of Furniture*, is open to a page showing a small Queen Anne highboy. The final issue of *Home Furniture* lies underneath the book, along with a scattering of shop drawings showing a pair of side tables with molded ovolo corners.

Styrofoam coffee cups and a plate of sweet rolls stand between us. I notice that, although I have long since gulped my coffee (and a pair of glazed doughnuts), Mark hasn't taken so much as a single sip of coffee.

The showroom opens up over my left shoulder. There, against the wall, Mark has positioned several examples of his period-inspired casework. A cherry highboy with madrone burl veneered drawer fronts dominates the arrangement. A reproduction of a Chippendale side chair, patterned after one made in Philadelphia in the eighteenth century by Thomas Affleck, stands to the left of the highboy. A Duncan Phyfe-inspired coffee table stands between them. Although these pieces are for sale, their most important function is to acquaint potential customers with the quality of the work done by the Boston Woodworking Company.

Mark is tall, dark-haired, slim. Like his voice, his hands are relaxed, resting on the tabletop as we speak, lifting occasionally to indicate a set of dimensions or to sketch a curve in the air with his forefinger. His wife, Margaret, who works at a nearby personal computer, is blonde, with a quick, magnetic smile.

I notice that Mark and Margaret say "we" when they talk about the Boston Woodworking Company, although it's Mark who does the woodworking. However, as I later learn, Margaret, a schoolteacher by day, is intimately involved in the running of this business. She is the one who keeps the books. It strikes me that she may also be the one who works most diligently to market the work issuing from their business.

Later, in the main room of Mark's shop, as my photographer positions her lights and Mark talks to a customer, Margaret and I stand off to one side. We talk about advertising, about the usefulness of brochures and catalogs, about woodworking shows, about other craftsmen. She is very knowledgeable, and she listens carefully. I have the sense that somewhere inside she's recording everything I say.

Children in America don't dream about someday becoming woodworkers. Instead, they dream about playing professional basketball or football, about becoming gymnasts or figure skaters. Like their idols, they want to experience life in the public eye, each moment lived to the accompaniment of ringing applause.

But eventually, most are weaned from this dream, and they look for other mountains to conquer. Some enter the work force directly after high school, taking jobs in offices and manufacturing plants. Others go to college and become teachers or doctors or businessmen. And a few, usually after some years of doing something else, decide to become craftsmen, to build careers out of taking material into their hands and, with it, fashioning the goods that will add texture and richness to the lives of their clients.

As a child, Mark Arnold didn't dream of someday becoming a woodworker. It was, instead, a destination he reached only after making a number of detours and false starts. But there were early experiences that planted the seed.

First, there was the presence in his home of woodworking tools. His father, a gentleman farmer, maintained a machine-tool-oriented woodshop in the basement of his home, using this machinery to do the rough work required by the upkeep of the farm's fences and outbuildings.

And second, even more important, there was the presence of material. When Mark was ten years old, a power company approached his father about running a line across the family's land, a project that would require the removal of a number of trees. Mark's father agreed but only under the condition that the power company have all the timber sawn up into lumber. The result was that, at a very young age, Mark had a ready supply of hardwood with which he felt free to experiment.

This fortuitous combination of tools and material during his childhood grafted onto Mark's psyche a set of experiences to which he would return again and again before finally setting himself up as a professional cabinetmaker.

After graduating from high school, Mark enrolled at Ohio State University, without any clearly defined career goals. There, after meeting some people from France and finding himself drawn to them, he began to focus his studies on French literature and the French language. This was a decision which, surprisingly, led him into a situation in which he found himself once again facing issues of woodworking and craftsmanship.

Mark explains: "While I was in school, one of my professors told me about this program in which you could go to the south of France and work for several weeks in the summer. Basically, in exchange for your work, you got food and lodging. I thought it was a great opportunity since I was planning to go to France anyway. So I got hold of the U.S. contact person and paid my dues and ended up going there.

"During my time in France, I got to know the owner of the chateau, who was a lawyer in Paris. The chateau was a family possession, something called a Gascon fortress. But it was just a big pile of rocks.

"Over the past twenty-five years, each summer he would get together volunteers to try and fix the place up. Every summer while I was in college, I ended up working in France. And while I worked on the chateau, I looked at other chateaus within the region. And it was the woodwork that most fascinated me.

"Some of the work I did on the chateau was just tuck-pointing stone walls—stuff like that—but I did have the opportunity to cut some mortise-and-tenon joints for a wood hand railing."

Back in the United States, Mark graduated from Ohio State University in 1990 with a degree in French language and literature. "Why French?" Mark poses the question before I can ask it. "I guess it's because I had enough credit hours in that area to graduate."

Although he eventually became a woodworking student at the prestigious North Bennet Street School in Boston, Massachusetts, Mark didn't enroll there immediately after graduation from OSU. In fact, at the time of his graduation, he hadn't even heard

Mark Arnold carves a scroll in his shop in Powell, Ohio.
Photographer:
Peggy Corbin

of the North Bennet Street School.

He first tried several other niches in the field of craft work, working briefly at Ohio Plate Glass, then later at Columbus Wood Products, a company that manufactures doors and moldings. "At first I was excited about being hired at Columbus Wood Products because I thought I'd get an opportunity to do some nice woodworking, but that was probably the dullest job I've ever had. I stood in front of a glorified table saw and just ran boards through it all day long, eight hours a day, five days a

week. After a couple of months, I could see the writing on the wall.

"So I decided to quit there and was immediately hired by a general contractor, Gary Porteus. He did some pretty nice work in Bexley (a Columbus suburb) and some of the other ritzy parts of town. I worked for him for three or four years. And I worked my way up to finish carpenter so I was doing some of the nicer stuff."

Although he enjoyed the time he spent working for Gary Porteus, he eventually realized that this was another job that wasn't quite right for

MARK ARNOLD: REVISITING THE GOLDEN AGE OF AMERICAN FURNITURE

him. Too often, he found himself on an icy roof in mid-December nailing rafters and sheeting into place. He wanted to get down off the roof and inside, where it was warmer; and just as important, he wanted work that demanded a greater level of precision and artistry.

"In the back of *Fine Woodworking*, they list different sources for instruction, so I wrote away to several of those and scheduled appointments. I looked at three different schools that offered a gamut of types of study. One was the Worcester Center for Crafts in Worcester, Massachusetts. I thought it looked like a really nice program. One of the requirements of their program for woodworking was that you take courses in some of the other disciplines, maybe glass working or metal working. That appealed to me because I've always liked stained glass, and I liked the idea of incorporating that into my work. Plus I thought I might use metalworking to make my own hardware.

"Then I went to the North Bennet Street School, and as soon as I took the tour of the building, I knew that was where I was going to end up, regardless of what the next place looked like."

Two names inevitably appear on anybody's short list of American woodworking schools. One, in Northern California, is The College of the Redwoods. This school, run by James Krenov, teaches classical skills in the context of contemporary designs. The other, the North Bennet Street School, in Boston, also teaches classical skills, but there the context is American period furniture.

NBSS's two-year program begins with an intensive six-week drafting course, during which students draw twenty woodworking joints to full scale, as well as five or six full-scale pieces in different styles. Then, after completing the drafting portion of the program, students are instructed in the fundamentals of hand-tool woodworking. Mark explains: "You learn how to tune up your hand planes, how to sharpen your chisels, how to get a card scraper to work properly.

"Then once a week, there is a day in the machine room. A lot of people think the school does only hand-tool work, but they also have a machine shop. That's an important part of modern woodworking—knowing how to change the knives on a planer, how to make your fence parallel to the blade on a table saw."

This work in the area of drawing, tool maintenance and tool operation takes up almost half of the first year at NBSS. Then, at the conclusion of this preparatory work, students are asked to design and build their own tool chests. Recognizing the ambition typical of the NBSS student, the staff places limits on the complexity of the tool chests. Mark explains: "You're given some parameters. They don't want you to build the Taj Mahal of tool chests, but they also want you to

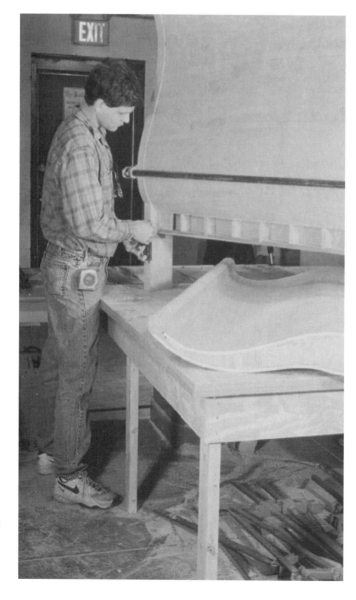

When time permits, Mark Arnold works on speculative pieces like this sleigh bed.
Photographer:
Peggy Corbin

build something nice for your first real piece of furniture."

After the completion of the tool chest, the students choose one each of the three primary types of furniture: a chair, a table and a casepiece. For his casepiece, Mark chose to build a cherry highboy with madrone veneer drawer fronts, a highboy closely modeled after one in Albert Sack's book *Fine Points of Furniture*. (This is the highboy now standing in the showroom of his shop.)

Creation of a scaled drawing was one of the many challenges posed by this casepiece, as the photo in Sack's book measures only 3″×5″ and includes no measurements and no information about the joinery in the original highboy. But perhaps the most complex aspect of this project was something Mark added, almost as an afterthought: a secret drawer hidden behind the cornice. "I could have made a solid cornice, but it was the last piece I built at NBSS, and I still had a month to go so I thought: 'Why not?'"

Instructor criticism of student work is one of the key elements in the NBSS program, offering students detailed feedback about their progress. Although Mark felt that some students might have taken offense at the criticism directed at their work, Mark took it "with a grain of salt," recognizing it wasn't directed at him but at his work. This criticism could focus on technical matters—perhaps an insufficient tenon length. It could also address aesthetic issues, as could be the case with an incompletely expressed curve in a cabriole leg. "Lance Patterson, who's the head instructor for the school, is notorious for seeing a missing hidden line (a hidden line is one that reveals a concealed detail, for instance a mortise-and-tenon joint) from across the room."

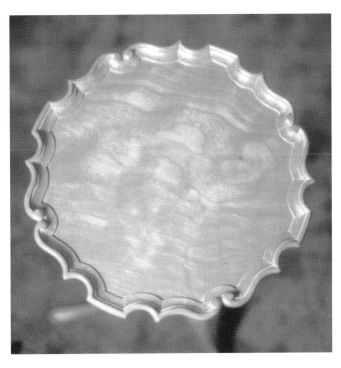

This piecrust candlestand in Mark Arnold's showroom is made from American cherry.
Photographer:
Peggy Corbin

One of the pieces Mark built during his time there did receive some criticism. Although most of the student-built work is based on specific period originals, one of Mark's projects—a low veneered table with Federal characteristics—was sufficiently different from any period original that it raised a few NBSS eyebrows. "It was so dissimilar from anything anybody had made before that some of the instructors thought it was kind of odd. Obviously it was in the Federal style because of the veneer work, but it didn't really look like anything that was built during the Federal period in America. This was because of the choice of woods and the table's shape."

Mark is quick to point out that although questions about his table were raised, the instructors didn't disapprove. "You see, there were students there from Venezuela, from Germany. The student body was so diverse you couldn't fit everybody in the same box. There were students building Beidermeyer furniture, plantation furniture from South Africa. As long as the piece had in it some essentials—

Western-style joinery, for example—the instructors didn't really have a problem with it.

"The school does have a reputation for being very traditional, but there is some room within that tradition."

A chairmaker can set up shop with nothing more than an armload of hand tools and a lathe, but the type of woodworking Mark learned at NBSS requires expensive machinery, as well as a generous selection of hand tools. Therefore, tooling was one of his first concerns after setting up his current shop in a small industrial park north of Columbus, Ohio. "I had some equipment already. While I worked for Gary Porteus, I made decent money, and I was able to buy a few things. But once I moved back, I needed a better planer (he bought an SCMI 20″ Formula I). I also bought a Multico mortiser, a Baldor grinder."

He also needed work.

Although he now advertises in the suburban papers on Columbus's north side, Mark initially sought work by contacting friends and acquaintances. "I put the word out that I was doing custom woodworking. I got back in touch with the contractor I'd been working for, and he sent a couple of jobs my way. Some friends of the family needed some kitchen cabinet doors." Although not the kind of work for which he had trained, it did bring in much-needed cash.

Mark and his wife also did a number of regional shows in an effort to put his work before the public. "Last year we did Winterfair (held in Columbus, Ohio, during the first weekend after Thanksgiving). Also we've done the Home Decorating and Remodeling Show at the State Fairgrounds (held in September) in Columbus two years in a row. We've also turned out to do some other shows, some of which turned out really well, some of which were a bust. At the Findlay Area Arts Festival, we won Best of Show for our booth."

Mark confesses that it's sometimes difficult to determine whether or not doing a particular show actually translates into business for The Boston Woodworking Company. "We haven't sold much out of our booth at any show, although this past year at the Remodeling Show, we did sell a pair of tiger maple tables. And then at the last show we did, the Artistry in Wood show in Dayton, where we also won Best of Show, we sold another tiger maple table. And at our first year of the Remodeling Show, we got a commission for a queen-size sleigh bed. I don't know if we got any commissions from this past year's show, but we have gotten a lot of inquiries."

There are a half-dozen pieces in Mark's showroom, all done on speculation. While he likes having them to

This sand-shaded fan is one of the signature details of Mark Arnold's veneer work.
Photographer: Peggy Corbin

show potential customers, they are all currently for sale. "The whole reason for making a piece is to sell it, but we also like having something in the showroom. It isn't the stuff in here that's our bread and butter. It's the stuff out there—" He gestures at the finishing room next door in which there were several birch plywood library cabinets awaiting a coat of aniline dye. "This—" He indicates the highboy, the veneered demilune table, the Chippendale side chair, "—is to show people what we can do, the different types of materials, the different types of joinery."

Experience has taught Mark that there is a complex psychology involved in closing a big-ticket reproduction sale. "It takes a couple of different things for a client to spend the kind of money required by work of this type. Obviously, they have to have that kind of money, but they also have to know what they're looking at and appreciate what they're looking at. Those two things alone, however, don't always end up in a commission. The third element is the desire to have the piece so much that

they're willing to part with the money. I mean I like the looks of a Jaguar, but even if I could afford one, I might not buy one."

Running a business is the one area of deficiency Mark notes in his training at NBSS. "They did offer a week-long workshop on the ins-and-outs of running your own business, but I think the school didn't really do its best in this area.

"But," he continues, "it's not a business school. And a lot of the people who go there aren't going to make a living at it. That's not why they're going there. They just want the knowledge. They just want to know so they can go home and produce really nice stuff in their basement workshops. A lot of them are retired. They don't need to make a living."

As a result, Mark and Margaret have been teaching themselves. This is an area in which Margaret, in particular, has exerted considerable effort, reading the available literature on the subject, keeping The Boston Woodworking Company's books, helping Mark with the process of do-

ing shows and meeting the public. These are efforts Mark appreciates. "I'm actually running this business with a lot of help from my family. As you can see, Margaret—" He indicates his wife, who smiles from her position at the computer. "—is doing our books right now. She takes care of a lot of things around here, as do her mother and father."

Mark's workday begins at 8:30 A.M., although doors aren't officially open until 9:00. He uses that first half hour to make sure his employee (Jim Bowman, Margaret's brother-in-law) has everything he needs to get through the day. Mark then spends some time on the phone with customers or suppliers. Then finally, after his employee has gotten under way, Mark turns his attention to whatever high-style piece he has currently under construction.

This is a method of operation with which he is very comfortable. "I don't want to get so big that I lose track of what's going on in the shop. I like to keep an eye on the quality of things because that's what we're trying to build the business on. We bill ourselves as the alternative to mass-produced furniture.

"If I ever did get to the point where I had a couple of employees, I could maybe think about producing a line of furniture, although I probably wouldn't make every piece in the line the same."

He contrasts his approach with that practiced by Thomas Moser, David T. Smith and Eldred Wheeler. "These are companies making nice furniture from solid hardwood with hand-cut dovetails. But each piece looks the same. Since they pretty much pay for the design costs of a piece by producing so many, they can sell them cheaper. I've seen a highboy similar to mine in curly maple by Eldred Wheeler for about $3,600. I

Like many of his contemporaries, Mark Arnold's shop employs a mix of hand and machine tool operations.
Photographer:
Peggy Corbin

would need a good bit more to reproduce the same piece.

"I spent about four weeks building that highboy. About one week of that was spent getting the cornice drawer, making sure that worked right. There's a lot of little details—like the veneered cove molding on the cornice, the herringbone banding on the drawer fronts, which was all handmade. People can usually tell the difference these details make, but sometimes getting them to pay for those details is another matter."

Few contemporary makers of high-style reproductions would be willing to trade places with the eighteenth- and early nineteenth-century craftsmen who originally produced classic period furniture. Few would be willing to work under the wavering light of candles through the long, dark days of winter. Fewer still would be willing to return to the brutal labor

of the pit saw. But there is a growing awareness that there was much that was right about the shop procedures used by those period-era craftsmen. When joinery and detailing are given the close scrutiny hand work requires, there is an evident difference in the quality of the finished piece.

Traditions are sometimes handed down from father to son, mother to daughter, and on, down through the generations. But not all traditions are dependent on this biological lineage. There are also traditions of sensibility that can be handed down from teacher to student, even when the lives of that teacher and that student are separated by centuries. In this way, contemporary builders of hand-detailed period reproductions, like Mark Arnold, are connected to the tradition of the John Goddards, the Duncan Phyfes, and the Thomas Afflecks of the golden age of American furniture.

TABLES

Artist Jake
Type of object hall table
Approximate size in inches 31×54×16
Material bird's-eye maple, curly maple, koa
Estimated cost of material $310
Estimated hours of labor 16
Price $1,100
Photographer Tony Grant

Q: **Would you recommend a career in woodworking to others?**

A: 87% of the contributors said "Yes."

" *The most difficult part of making a living as a woodworker is selling your work for enough to provide for a family, but this is in direct relationship to being satisfied with less junk.*"

CURTIS BUCHANAN,
JONESBOROUGH, TN

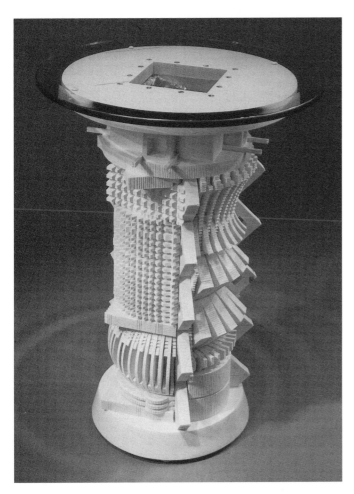

Artist Po Shun Leong
Type of object table
Approximate size in inches 26×18
Material bleached maple, glass
Estimated cost of material $125
Estimated hours of labor 16
Price $2,500
Photographer Po Shun Leong

Artist Jonathan W. McLean
Type of object tea table
Approximate size in inches $26 \times 32 \times 22$
Material mahogany
Estimated cost of material $200
Estimated hours of labor 160
Price $5,500
Photographer Lance Patterson

Artist Kerry Pierce

Type of object table

Approximate size in inches $22^{11}/_{16} \times 24\frac{1}{2} \times 14\frac{5}{8}$

Material curly maple, cherry, pine

Estimated cost of material $25

Estimated hours of labor 30

Price $600

Photographer Adam Blake

Artist Barry Sweeney

Type of object hall table

Approximate size in inches $34 \times 47 \times 16$

Material mahogany, madrone burl

Estimated cost of material $200

Estimated hours of labor 40

Price $1,200

Photographer Lance Patterson

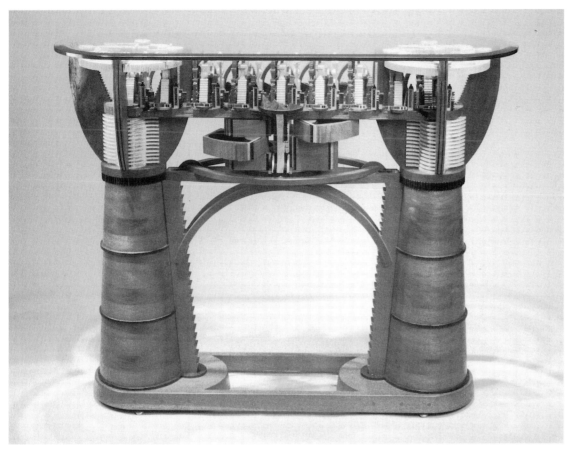

Artist Po Shun
Leong

Type of object table

Approximate size in
inches 36×48×16

Material Hawaiian
koa, wenge,
mahogany,
maple, ebony,
pink ivorywood

Estimated cost of
material $250

Estimated hours of
labor 32

Price $12,500

Photographer Po Shun
Leong

Artist Jake

Type of object hall
table

Approximate size in
inches 31×54×18

Material jatoba,
walnut

Estimated cost of
material $180

Estimated hours of
labor 35

Price $1,800

Photographer Tony
Grant

Artist Mark Arnold
Type of object pair of tables
Approximate size in inches (each) 27×17×14
Material tiger maple, period brasses
Estimated cost of material (each) $90
Estimated hours of labor (each) 20
Price (each) $750
Photographer LaJuan Spencer

Artist Jake
Type of object coffee table
Approximate size in inches 17×48×19
Material cherry, curly maple
Estimated cost of material $160
Estimated hours of labor 20
Price $1,500
Photographer Tony Grant

Artist Mark Arnold
Type of object candle stand
Approximate size in inches $25 \times 13\frac{1}{2}$
Material curly cherry, cherry
Estimated cost of material $50
Estimated hours of labor 40
Price $1,000
Photographer Lance Patterson

> " *In the early years, I was un-aware of all the opportuni-ties, which made our situation inse-cure. Nowadays, the difficult parts are learning how to enjoy the financial re-wards and keeping thoughts of the next woodworking project out of one's mind.*"
>
> **PO SHUN LEONG, WINNETKA, CA**

Artist Jake
Type of object coffee table
Approximate size in inches $17 \times 50 \times 20$
Material fiddleback English sycamore, ebonized mahogany
Estimated cost of material $150
Estimated hours of labor 20
Price $900
Photographer Tony Grant

Artist Kerry Pierce

Type of object table

Approximate size in inches 23¾×23½×17

Material walnut, pine

Estimated cost of material $75

Estimated hours of labor 30

Price $600

Photographer Adam Blake

Artist Jake

Type of object tables

Approximate size in inches 25×11×11 and 29×11×11

Material bird's eye maple, Peruvian walnut, cherry

Estimated cost of material (each) $90

Estimated hours of labor (each) 14

Price (each) $650

Photographer Tony Grant

Artist Po Shun Leong

Type of object table

Approximate size in inches $36 \times 48 \times 16$

Material mahogany, cherry, wenge, maple, buckeye burl

Estimated cost of material $250

Estimated hours of labor 32

Price $12,500

Photographer Po Shun Leong

Barry Sweeney's Computer/Library Desk

Barry Sweeney's computer/library desk was not built as a commission. It was, instead, a piece done on speculation that will appear in a brochure Barry is now in the process of preparing.

This desk is a result of Barry's desire to solve some of the problems he sees in commercially available computer desks. He wanted a desk large enough to be used as a library table, with a slide-out keyboard shelf to carry and conceal the keyboard and the mouse, and a keyboard shelf covered in leather, making a mouse pad unnecessary. He also wanted a desk attractive enough to look at home in an executive office setting.

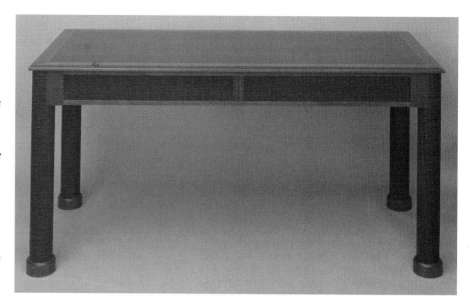

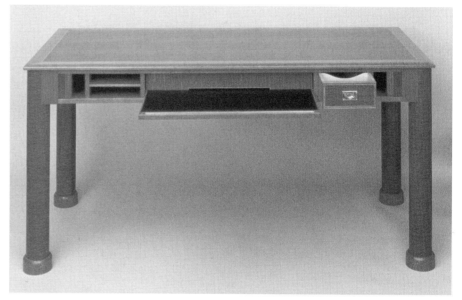

Artist Barry Sweeney
Type of object computer desk
Approximate size in inches 36 × 72 × 32
Material pomelle sapelle, fiddleback mahogany, lacewood
Estimated cost of material $1,200
Estimated hours of labor 160
Price $8,500
Photographer Lance Patterson

Jonathan McLean's Bombé Desk

Although its basic forms are taken from a piece in the Winterthur museum, Jonathan McLean's bombé desk is not a reproduction of any specific period original. Jonathan's desk has a lower writing surface than the Winterthur original, and the interior of his desk—the pigeonhole area—is not a reproduction. It is an arrangement Jonathan created to suit his own tastes.

"I did my own drawings," he explains, "although I never saw the actual piece at Winterthur. There's pictures of that piece in an old Antiques *magazine. In fact, there's two of these desks in that article. The magazine did a comparison. My drawings were based on those photos."*

The bombé desk wasn't done on commission. (In fact, it is still in his possession.) He explains that every year he tries to do one or two speculative pieces, like this desk, simply because he wants to do them. "If I wait for a commission on a piece like this, I might never get it."

The price on this desk, $26,500, is the price he would have charged for the desk in 1991, the year in which he built it. "If somebody walked in today and offered me $26,500, I'm not sure I'd take it. That piece has actually made me more money by just being around.

I won the American Woodworker *contest with it in 1992 or 1993, and I've showed it in several shows. There's a picture of it in a recent issue of* Early American Homes.*"*

Artist Jonathan W. McLean
Type of object desk
Approximate size in inches $43 \times 37 \times 20$
Material mahogany, poplar, brasses
Estimated cost of material $575
Estimated hours of labor 750
Price $26,500
Photographer Lance Patterson

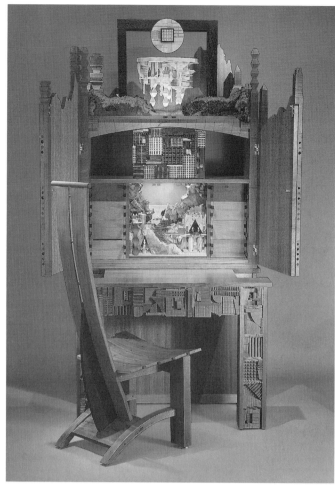

Artist Po Shun Leong

Type of object desk and chair

Approximate size in inches $84 \times 30 \times 20$

Material mahogany, various woods

Estimated cost of material $500

Estimated hours of labor 120

Price $25,000

Photographer Po Shun Leong

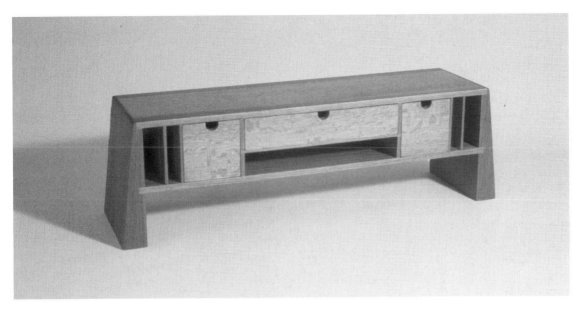

Artist Chris Kamm
Type of object desk
  secretary
Approximate size in
  inches $10 \times 34 \times 10$
Material white oak,
  Sierra oak
Estimated cost of
  material $35
Estimated hours of labor
  6
Price $345
Photographer Jon
  Lucich

Artist John Hartcorn
Type of object desk
Approximate size in inches $30 \times 45 \times 25$
Material mahogany, mahogany veneer,
  maple
Estimated cost of material $500
Estimated hours of labor 170
Price $6,500
Photographer Lance Patterson

Artist Brent Karner

Type of object table

Approximate size in inches 30 × 48 × 16

Material cherry, curly maple

Estimated cost of material $47

Estimated hours of labor 10

Price $598

Photographer Brent Karner

Artist Kerry Pierce

Type of object table

Approximate size in inches 30 × 28 × 19¾

Material cherry, pine, walnut

Estimated cost of material $75

Estimated hours of labor 25

Price $600

Photographer Adam Blake

JOE GRAHAM: WINDSOR CHAIRMAKER

When I pull into the driveway of Joe Graham's shop, I leave the engine running for a few moments and put my nose against one of the air conditioning vents. It's 91 degrees and my shirt, soaked through, clings to my back like a second skin.

Today is the fifth and final day of one of Joe Graham's Windsor chairmaking workshops. During the previous four days, his students have been busy wresting chair parts from logs using riving and shaping tools with which they'd likely had little or no prior experience—all during one of the hottest weekends Ohio has seen in years.

I wonder if, inside, I will find woodworkers turned mean by the heat and hard work.

Joe's wife meets me at the door to the shop. She smiles, introduces herself and shakes my hand. She leads me inside.

The shop isn't as hot as I'd imagined it would be. On both sides of the large main workroom, barn doors have been pulled back, allowing the free movement of air.

Joe Graham, wearing only a pair of shorts, stands in the center of the room, bare feet on a carpet of wood shavings. Ranged around him are four work stations, each equipped with a sturdy lathe and shaving horse. Thick planks of cherry, poplar and walnut stand on end along the back wall of the shop.

At three of the work stations, men are busy fitting spindles into the backs of the Windsors they'd assembled during the week. I look from face to face. No sign of crankiness here. These men are actually smiling.

For most of the afternoon, I sit on a comfortable Windsor settee and watch as the three students, with Joe's advice and encouragement, carry out the tricky work of aligning and drilling the mortises for the spindles that will make up the back of their Windsors.

Each technique is first demonstrated by Joe with the workshop participants gathered around. An informal question-and-answer period follows, after which the students drift off to their own chairs where they put in practice what they have just learned.

It is clear that, even in the day's tremendous heat, each of the students is enjoying himself. Yes, there is serious intent, but there is also laughter and, as the chairs move closer to completion, a growing sense of pride and accomplishment.

One of the key elements in Joe's instructions to his students is the notion of "building by eye," a concept he extends to every step in the chairmaking process. For example, when placing the reference spindles for the bow backs, the students are encouraged to align them by eye, to place them tentatively into position and then judge the rightness of that position by stepping back and relying on their intuition.

For woodworkers accustomed to working from meticulously drawn plans, this can be disconcerting, but as Joe explains, it can open up the practice of chairmaking: "It permits an intimate connection with each of the chair's parts. It engages the craftsman with the work, making every chair an expression of that person's aesthetic."

On its simplest level, this is nothing more than an acknowledgement of the fact that hand work has irregularities, that the vase on one chair leg might have a maximum diameter an eighth inch less than the vase of the matching leg on the other side of the chair. But on another level, the notion of "building by eye" frees the chairmaker from the need to mimic the regularities of machine work, allowing him to focus on the creation of a beautiful artifact.

Seven years into his career as a union carpenter in the Cleveland area, Joe began to look for something that could offer him a greater measure of independence. Long an admirer of the home designs of Frank Lloyd Wright (Joe's own home is a solar hemicycle, patterned after Wright's Jacob House), he decided to study architecture.

His first stop was Cleveland State University where he spent a year taking engineering courses. He then transferred to Kent State University, enrolling in the school of architecture. There, however, his enthusiasm waned as, in his judgment, the possibility of making a living as a designer of homes seemed increasingly unrealistic. He then left Kent State, returning to Cleveland, where he again took up carpentry.

Custom kitchen work seemed another possible route to independence, and for several years, he attempted to shift his work from carpentry to the design and construction of custom kitchens. In another community, he might have succeeded, but his hometown, Jefferson, Ohio, is a small town in a rural area on the south shore of Lake Erie, and there simply wasn't enough demand for this type of work.

Then, in 1982, an announcement in *Fine Woodworking* for a Windsor chairmaking workshop given by Michael Dunbar suggested still another possibility. "I didn't even know what a Windsor chair was," Joe explains. "I just wanted to be independent. Also, I thought the experience might make me a better woodworker, even if I couldn't make a living selling chairs."

Then, at Dunbar's workshop, Joe found himself drawn to the chairs themselves. "They were sturdy and honest, obviously refined over the years. They were objects developed by tradition, and that tradition was written in the first chair I built."

Most contemporary Windsors are built in one of two ways. Some chairmakers have simplified the chair's forms to facilitate machine work and mass production. Others follow a more laborious route to the finished chair. They build their Windsors in essentially the same way they have been built for hundreds of years, relying almost entirely on hand tools. Joe falls into this second group, and some of the difficulties he experienced in establishing his business resulted from his decision to avoid production techniques.

"I don't do it alone. My wife, Barbara, and my son, Charlie, help out with spindle making, sanding, finishing. But every chair is individually built with the lion's share of the work done with hand tools. This makes it necessary to sell the chairs for high prices, but even at those prices it has been a struggle."

In 1987, seeking to expand his business, Joe attended a workshop sponsored by the Ohio Designer Craftsmen led by twig chairmaker Dan Muck. Joe then began to build twig chairs with the intent of moving into the East Coast art market. Although he was pleased with his designs, he found it difficult to make money with this line. "Maybe I lost patience, but after disappointing sales at the Smithsonian Craft Show (then called the Washington Craft Show), I refocused on my Windsors."

In 1990, with eight years of chairmaking experience behind him, Joe felt confident enough to teach the skills he'd acquired, and over the next three years, he taught a number of workshops at a bed-and-breakfast in Geneva-on-the-Lake. There, with

the assistance of Earl and Grace Hoffa, he instructed 38 students in the art and mystery of chairmaking.

"From the beginning, the workshops were very rewarding. The sense of accomplishment experienced by my chairbuilders was obvious." Although many highly skilled woodworkers have taken Joe's workshops, there have been many others who

With a wooden-bodied spokeshave, Joe Graham refines the shape of a Windsor chair seat in his shop near Jefferson, Ohio.

Photographer: Kerry Pierce

Joe Graham uses a compass plane to surface the concave interior of a Windsor chair seat.

Photographer: Kerry Pierce

make a living with hand tools," he explains. "It's been physically demanding work over a long time. After a while you learn to understand why there was this push for mechanization.

"Still," he adds, "hand tool work shouldn't be lost. Even if you make only one chair in your life, it teaches you something about working with wood you couldn't learn with machine tools."

The defining characteristics of the Windsor are dictated by history: the turned legs and stretcher, the scooped seat, the shaved spindles. But through the "continual refinement of line," Joe has put his own signature on this form. His Windsors are not the result of an attempt to replicate any specific eighteenth-century model. They are, instead, an attempt to create something new that is still deeply rooted in the Windsor tradition. Joe explains: "The beauty of the tradition is the capacity for individual expression that results from the skillful manipulation of hand-held tools." It's the freedom he finds in this manipulation that allows him to embellish this form in a way that differentiates his chairs from those of his predecessors.

Although its seat suggests a Windsor, Joe's Lenox chairs are something different. Named for the township in which he lives, the Lenox chairs are Joe's own creations. Neither the stretcher nor the legs are turned. They are, instead, cut out with a saber saw, then brought to their finished shapes with a drawknife and spokeshave. For lower-back support, the spindles are steambent to conform to the shape of the human body. One other distinguishing characteristic is the exaggerated splay of the legs (a feature Joe has also included in some of his more

"bring nothing more than a strong desire to build a Windsor, who do it and are awed by their accomplishment." Certainly, for many students, the pleasure they experience is pride in newly acquired skills. But Joe cites one other reason for his students' satisfaction: "It requires physical power to build a Windsor, and that chair becomes a symbol of your physical power."

Although he still finds enjoyment in the construction of his own chairs, Joe sees the workshops as his future and has moved that operation to his own residence, building sleeping rooms for his students, a bath and a large workroom. "It's difficult to

JOE GRAHAM: WINDSOR CHAIRMAKER

With an inshave, Joe Graham cleans up the tool marks left by the adze.
Photographer: Kerry Pierce

traditional Windsors). The Lenox chair is Joe's attempt to create a new form still connected to the Windsor tradition.

However, Joe's series of twig chairs presented him with his stiffest design challenge. They relied on "found" shapes and were not shaped with the same tools with which Joe customarily works. "They were grueling to construct. I remember endless piles of interesting twigs selected from the woods in day-long excursions. I remember neck aches from circling trees, looking up through the branches silhouetted against the sky. And the endless taping together of pieces in search of something that looked natural but still chairlike.

"It was agony, but I was gratified by the result."

Although Joe is firmly entrenched in the centuries-old tradition of Wind-

sor chairmaking, he has made some concessions to the twentieth century in his methods of work. He uses an electric drill and spade bit to make his mortises. He turns legs and stretchers on a lathe powered by an electric motor. But for the operation most critical to the Windsor, for the shaping of the seat, Joe relies on the same hand tools that have traditionally shaped Windsor chair seats.

Other contemporary chairmakers have developed machine techniques for this operation, allowing not only quicker but also less skill-intensive production work, which opens the possibility of having this task accomplished with hired help. I ask Joe why he hasn't taken this approach.

He explains that noise is one consideration. Anyone who has operated a shaper or router can appreciate the quiet of hand-tool shaping. Also, Joe finds the uniformity inherent in ma-

chine production unappealing. He prizes the variations typical of handmade parts, as they provide incontrovertible proof of the craftsman's presence in the chairmaking process.

"Also," he adds, "the tools have a definite appeal—the way they look, feel. They're unusual. They're tools not everybody knows."

To illustrate, he tells a story: "One night several years ago I was working late in the shop. It was snowing and the roads were bad. About 11:00 this kid put his car in the ditch. I guess my shop light was the only one on along this stretch of road because he came to the shop for help. I was shaping a chair seat when he knocked. I was using an adze, and he saw it laying on the bench when he came in.

"The kid went to school with my son, Charlie, and Charlie said the next day the kid was telling everybody about this axe murderer who'd helped him.

"I thought his comment was funny, but it does make a couple of points. Not everybody knows these tools. Most people can't tell an adze from an axe. And the tools are dangerous. To work properly, the adze must be sharp. And you use it between your feet. That takes a certain coordination. There's a dance you do with the adze."

Watching Joe shape a chair seat is a compelling experience. First, it is a process heavily laden with tradition. Although he claims no particular connection to eighteenth-century chairmakers, his handling of the adze, the inshave and the drawknife nevertheless evokes those craftsmen. Second, there is risk in the process—the adze is very sharp—and he drives it with great force into the seat blank. Last, this work involves an appealing balance of physical power and delicate control, an athleticism one doesn't expect to see in the woodshop.

Oak splits lay in the grass outside Joe Graham's shop. Bending stock for a set of Windsors was taken from this material.
Photographer: Kerry Pierce

CHAIRS

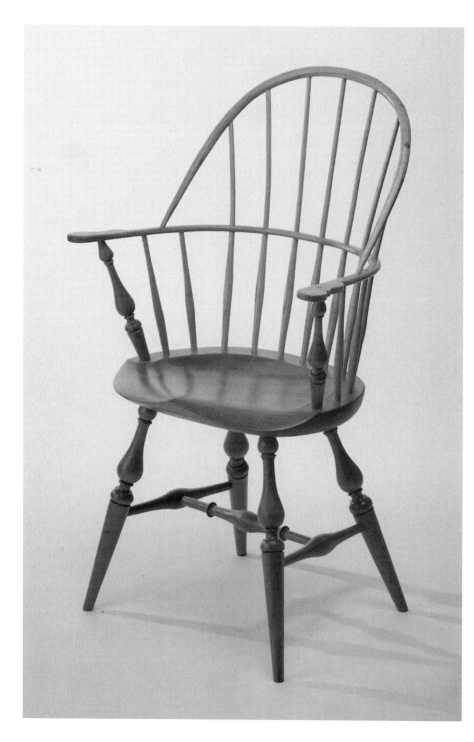

Artist David Wright
Type of object armchair
Approximate size in inches 39 × 24 × 21
Material cherry, red oak
Estimated cost of material $30
Estimated hours of labor 35
Price $785
Photographer Lee Thomas

Artist David Wright
Type of object rocking chair
Approximate size in inches $43 \times 28 \times 24$
Material poplar, red oak, maple
Estimated cost of material $40
Estimated hours of labor 45
Price $1,050
Photographer Lee Thomas

Artist David Wright
Type of object side chair
Approximate size in inches $39 \times 21 \times 23$
Material cherry, red oak
Estimated cost of material $25
Estimated hours of labor 25
Price $625
Photographer Lee Thomas

Artist Kerry Vesper
Type of object chair
Approximate size in inches $31 \times 32 \times 21$
Material cherry, luan plywood
Estimated cost of material $250
Estimated hours of labor 120
Price $3,000
Photographer Greg Masturakos

Artist Barry Sweeney
Type of object armchair
Approximate size in inches $42 \times 30 \times 30$
Material cherry, leather
Estimated cost of material $350
Estimated hours of labor 80
Price $4,500
Photographer Lance Patterson

Q: **How would you best describe your shop operations?**

A: 63% of the contributors said "A mix of hand- and power-tool operations."
20% said "Power-tool dominated."
17% said "Hand-tool dominated."

Artist Owen Rein
Type of object rocking chair
Approximate size in inches $45 \times 33 \times 24$
Material white oak, hickory, hickory bark
Estimated cost of material $5
Estimated hours of labor 55
Price $650
Photographer Larry McSpadden

Artist Owen Rein
Type of object rocking chair
Approximate size in inches $45 \times 33 \times 24$
Material white oak, walnut, hickory bark
Estimated cost of material $5
Estimated hours of labor 35
Price $450
Photographer Larry McSpadden

Artist Joe Graham
Type of object Welsh side chair
Approximate size in inches $36 \times 24 \times 22$
Material oak
Estimated cost of material $40
Estimated hours of labor 30
Price $550
Photographer Jerry Anthony

Artist Mike Dunbar
Type of object Windsor armchair
Approximate size in inches $37 \times 22 \times 24$
Material pine, maple, oak
Estimated cost of material $20
Estimated hours of labor 10
Price $650
Photographer Andrew Edgar

When asked about the most satisfying part of making a living as a woodworker, Curtis Buchanan gave this response:

“ *Early in the morning walking the 200 feet to my shop, checking on my tomatoes and beans along the way, stepping inside my door, and standing still for quite a few moments surveying the situation.*”

**CURTIS BUCHANAN,
JONESBOROUGH, TN**

Artist Mike Dunbar
Type of object Windsor side chair
Approximate size in inches $37 \times 21 \times 22$
Material pine, maple, oak
Estimated cost of material $20
Estimated hours of labor 8
Price $600
Photographer Andrew Edgar

Artist Mike Dunbar
Type of object Windsor writing armchair
Approximate size in inches $43 \times 31 \times 33$
Material pine, maple, oak
Estimated cost of material $20
Estimated hours of labor 11
Price $650
Photographer Andrew Edgar

Artist Mike Dunbar

Type of object Windsor armchair

Approximate size in inches $44 \times 27 \times 29$

Material pine, maple, oak, mahogany

Estimated cost of material $25

Estimated hours of labor 13

Price $850

Photographer Andrew Edgar

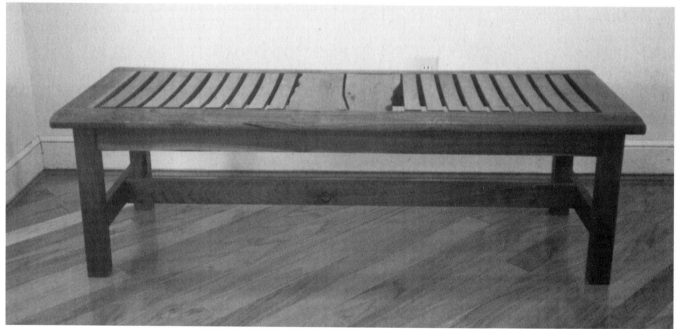

Artist Sal Cretella

Type of object bench

Approximate size in inches $16 \times 54 \times 20$

Material walnut

Estimated cost of material $140

Estimated hours of labor 20

Price $600

Photographer Sal Cretella

Artist Sal Cretella
Type of object bench
Approximate size in inches $41 \times 78 \times 24$
Material mahogany
Estimated cost of material $400
Estimated hours of labor 40
Price $1,900
Photographer Sal Cretella

Artist Curtis Buchanan
Type of object armchair
Approximate size in inches $35 \times 12 \times 12\frac{1}{2}$
Material red oak, sugar maple, pine
Estimated cost of materials $30
Estimated hours of labor 35
Price $850
Photographer Tom Pardue

Artist Curtis Buchanan
Type of object rocking chair
Approximate size in inches 44×17×18½
Material red oak, sugar maple, pine
Estimated cost of material $40
Estimated hours of labor 45
Price $1,275
Photographer Dan Robinson

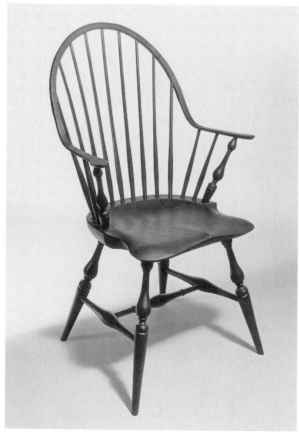

Artist Curtis Buchanan
Type of object armchair
Approximate size in inches 36×17×18½
Material red oak, pine, sugar maple
Estimated cost of material $40
Estimated hours of labor 35
Price $850
Photographer Tom Pardue

Q: **Was woodworking your first career choice?**

A: 69% of the contributors said "Yes."

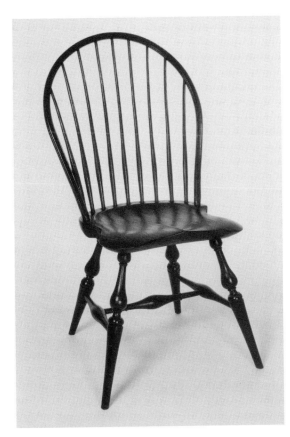

Artist Curtis Buchanan
Type of object side chair
Approximate size in inches $37 \times 17 \times 17$
Material red oak, sugar maple, pine
Estimated cost of material $40
Estimated hours of labor 30
Price $700
Photographer Tom Pardue

Artist Curtis Buchanan
Type of object armchair
Approximate size in inches $46 \times 15\frac{1}{2} \times 21$
Material red oak, pine, sugar maple
Estimated cost of material $40
Estimated hours of labor 50
Price $1,225
Photographer Dan Robinson

Artist Curtis Buchanan
Type of object settee
Approximate size in inches $37 \times 15\frac{1}{2} \times 41$
Material red oak, pine, sugar maple
Estimated cost of material $60
Estimated hours of labor 60
Photographer $1,675
Photographer Tom Pardue

Artist Joe Graham
Type of object rocking chair
Approximate size in inches $46 \times 36 \times 28$
Material walnut, oak
Estimated cost of material $60
Estimated hours of labor 45
Price $850
Photographer Jerry Anthony

> ❝ *After my time studies, I look at the finished piece and ask if I can get the price derived or not. I then usually bump the price up based on what I consider the 'right' price for it to sell rather quickly.*
>
> *"I can get a much higher price in my New York store than I can usually get at a fair."*
>
> **RICHARD ROTHBARD, SLATE HILL, NY**

Artist Owen Rein
Type of object stool
Approximate size in inches $28 \times 14 \times 14$
Material white oak, hickory, hickory bark
Estimated cost of material $1
Estimated hours of labor 9
Price $95
Photographer Larry McSpadden

Artist Owen Rein
Type of object sewing chair
Approximate size in inches $34 \times 15 \times 18$
Materials hickory, ebony, hickory bark
Estimated cost of material $1.50
Estimated hours of labor 15
Price $135
Photographer Larry McSpadden

Artist Kerry Pierce
Type of object armchairs
Approximate size in inches $43 \times 17 \times 23$
Material cherry, rush
Estimated cost of material (each) $80
Estimated hours of labor (each) 35
Price (each) $600
Photographer Kerry Pierce

Artist Kerry Pierce
Type of object rocking chair
Approximate size in inches $45 \times 31 \times 28$
Material cherry, Shaker tape
Estimated cost of material $100
Estimated hours of labor 25
Price $500
Photographer Kerry Pierce

> **"** *The most satisfying part of making a living as a woodworker? Cashing the check. And time spent in the woods not using a chain saw.*"
>
> **JOE GRAHAM, JEFFERSON, OH**

Artist Kerry Pierce
Type of object rocking chair
Approximate size in inches $47 \times 28 \times 29$
Material cherry, rattan splint
Estimated cost of material $55
Estimated hours of labor 27
Price $575
Photographer Dave Saunders

Artist Kerry Pierce
Type of object side chair
Approximate size in inches $41 \times 17 \times 23$
Material cherry, Shaker tape
Estimated cost of material $85
Estimated hours of labor 17
Price $350
Photographer Kerry Pierce

Artist Kerry Pierce
Type of object armchair
Approximate size in inches $41 \times 17 \times 22$
Material cherry, Shaker tape
Estimated cost of material $90
Estimated hours of labor 20
Price $375
Photographer Kerry Pierce

Artist Kerry Pierce
Type of object rocking chair
Approximate size in inches $45 \times 28 \times 24$
Material walnut, rattan splint
Estimated cost of materials $60
Estimated hours of labor 25
Price $500
Photographer Kerry Pierce

> " The most difficult part of being a woodworker is balancing my responsibilities as a father and husband with my needs and interests related to my work.
>
> "Equally—or even more difficult—is setting aside time as a self-employed person. It seems there are no weekends or holidays; every day is a potential work day."
>
> **NORM SARTORIUS, PARKERSBURG, WV**

Artist Kerry Pierce
Type of object armchairs
Approximate size in inches $42 \times 18 \times 24$
Material fiddleback maple, rattan splint
Estimated cost of material (each) $100
Estimated hours of labor (each) 20
Price (each) $475
Photographer Kerry Pierce

Artist Kerry Pierce
Type of object side chairs
Approximate size in inches $42 \times 17 \times 23$
Material fiddleback maple, Shaker tape
Estimated cost of material (each) $100
Estimated hours of labor (each) 18
Price (each) $450
Photographer Kerry Pierce

Artist Jonathan W. McLean
Type of object armchair
Approximate size in inches 44×19×23
Material cherry
Estimated cost of material $300
Estimated hours of labor 100
Price $3,500
Photographer Lance Patterson

Artist Beth Ann Harrington
Type of object side chair
Approximate size in inches 35×19½×19
Material cherry, basswood, madrone burl, ebony
Estimated cost of material $100
Estimated hours of labor 53
Price $2,000 (does not include upholstery)
Photographer Lance Patterson

Artist Mike Dunbar
Type of object Windsor armchair
Approximate size in inches $37 \times 21 \times 24$
Material pine, maple, oak
Estimated cost of material $20
Estimated hours of labor 11
Price $750
Photographer Andrew Edgar

> " *Certain pieces of furniture have more status. Stools have low status. Rockers have high status. Therefore an hour spent working on a rocker will yield more than an hour spent working on a stool.* "
>
> **JOE GRAHAM, JEFFERSON, OH**

Artist Joe Graham
Type of object armchair
Approximate size in inches $47 \times 28 \times 30$
Material walnut, oak
Estimated cost of material $60
Estimated hours of labor 45
Price $875
Photographer Jerry Anthony

Artist W. Richard Goehring
Type of object rocking chair
Approximate size in inches $42 \times 32 \times 22$
Material walnut, ebonized walnut, Shaker
    tape
Estimated cost of material $60
Estimated hours of labor 35 +
Price $825
Photographer W. R. Goehring

Artist Joe Graham
Type of object writing armchair
Approximate size in inches $48 \times 30 \times 35$
Material maple, poplar, oak
Estimated cost of material $60
Estimated hours of labor 50
Price $950
Photographer Jerry Anthony

Artist Joe Graham
Type of object armchair
Approximate size in inches 46 × 26 × 30
Material maple, poplar, oak
Estimated cost of material $50
Estimated hours of labor 40
Price $775
Photographer Jerry Anthony

Artist Curtis Buchanan
Type of object armchair
Approximate size in inches 45 × 18 × 19
Material red oak, sugar maple, pine
Estimated cost of material $40
Estimated hours of labor 40
Price $1,125
Photographer Dan Robinson

Artist Curtis Buchanan
Type of object chair
Approximate size in inches $36 \times 17 \times 16\frac{1}{2}$
Material red oak, sugar maple, pine
Estimated cost of material $40
Estimated hours of labor 40
Price $1,000
Photographer Tom Pardue

Artist Curtis Buchanan
Type of object armchairs
Approximate size in inches Left: $35 \times 12 \times 12\frac{1}{2}$
Right: $45 \times 18 \times 19$
Material red oak, pine, sugar maple
Estimated cost of material (each) $40
Estimated hours of labor (each) 40
Price (each) $1,125
Photographer Dan Robinson

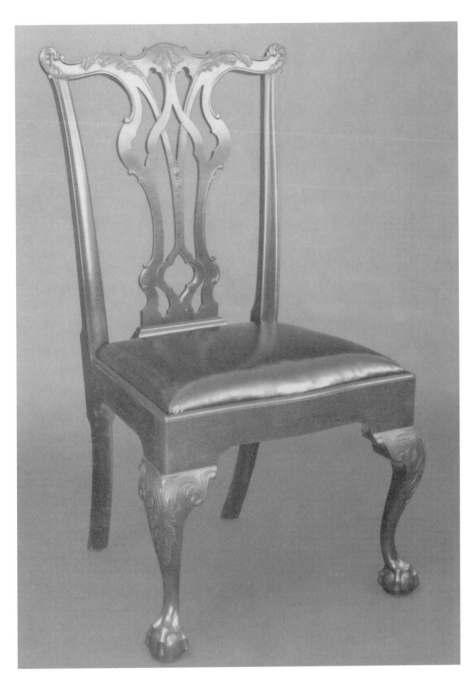

Artist Mark Arnold
Type of object side chair
Approximate size in inches 40½ × 22 × 24
Material mahogany, poplar, ash
Estimated cost of material $150
Estimated hours of labor 80
Price $2,800
Photographer Lance Patterson

Q: Do you see yourself remaining a woodworker until retirement?

A: 97% of the contributors said "Yes."

B.A. Harrington and Judith Hanson's Settle

B.A. Harrington and Judith Hanson share shop space in Medford, Massachusetts. They also, occasionally, share jobs. This settle, built several years ago on commission, was one of their earliest collaborations.

"It's not actually a reproduction," B.A. Harrington explains. "It's based on a piece made by a turn-of-the-century company called the Shop of the Crafters." The specifics of this design evolved from a photograph of the Shop-of-the-Crafters piece the customer showed B.A. and Judith. From that beginning, they created the piece shown here.

Like everyone who is new to the woodworking discipline, B.A. and Judith have struggled with the problem of setting prices. In fact, the price listed here for the piece, $5,200, is not the price their customer paid several years ago. "This piece was made at the beginning of our time as woodworkers. We actually didn't charge the listed price. $5,200 is the price that we arrived at later, the price that we would sell another one for."

B.A.'s current pricing strategy looks only at labor and materials, adding nothing for overhead and profit because as she explains, "I'm not that big an operation,

and my overhead is very low, and I'm still in the process of trying to figure out how to do this (make a living as a woodworker)."

To maintain a steady flow of money, B.A. waits tables two nights a week. "I waited tables for probably sixteen years now. That's how I put myself through school and then through trade school, to study furniture making, and I just kept the job. It's actually been a good set up. It's allowed me to not burn out on the woodworking. That means I don't have to take on projects I really don't want to do."

Artist Beth Ann Harrington (and Judith Hanson)
Type of object settle
Approximate size in inches $37 \times 59 \times 30$
Material white oak, various veneers
Estimated cost of material $400
Estimated hours of labor 160
Price $5,200
Photographer Lance Patterson

DAVID WRIGHT: THE VIRTUES OF SIMPLICITY

Over the past twenty-five years American woodworking has taken two very different courses. As mainstream woodworkers have made their operations more and more equipment intensive, filling their shops with ever more sophisticated machinery, other woodworkers have turned away from power equipment and have, instead, made shop operations more and more hand-tool intensive. For some in this second group, the motivation may be a desire to return to the perceived romance of eighteenth-century woodworking, but for others, this movement in the direction of hand-tool use is more than simple nostalgia; it is, in fact, an admission of the limitations and liabilities inherent in even the most sophisticated power equipment.

There is no question that power tools allow work to be done more quickly. With a planer, lumber can be dressed to a consistent thickness as fast as it can be fed into the machine. Power equipment allows a shop owner to hire relatively unskilled workers. After all, anyone can be taught to feed lumber into a planer. But only a skilled craftsman can transform a length of rough 4/4 material into a smoothly finished piece of 3/4 stock using nothing but hand planes, a pair of winding sticks and a straightedge.

But the power planer is noisy and dirty. When it runs, the shop is a mind-jangling place to work. Hand planes are, by contrast, quiet and clean. When they are in use, reflection is possible. In a quiet shop, it is possible to *think* about what one is doing. And it is this reflection, coupled with the sensitivity possible with the deft manipulation of hand tools, that has encouraged many contemporary woodworkers to turn away from the speed of power equipment and return to the subtleties of the drawknife, the spokeshave and carving gouges.

From the moment I arrive at David

Wright's home, I'm certain he belongs to the second group of craftsmen. His shop, a small, frame, one-car garage with a bit of a westward lean, isn't large enough to house a collection of expensive woodworking machinery. A modest hand-painted sign tacked to the front reads: "David Wright, Chairmaker." In the driveway, there is a heap of hickory splits covered now with snow.

As I approach the shop looking for a way in, the overhead door rises and David steps out to meet me. We shake hands. "C'mon in," he says. "Then I can shut the door and save some heat."

Inside, the building is even smaller than it looks from the outside. Along the east wall there is a workbench and a storage cabinet. A half-dozen thick cherry planks, soon to become chair seats, lean against the back wall. In one corner, there is a dusty ten-inch table saw. "I only use it to cut the notches for rockers," he explains later. Along the west wall, there is a large, antique band saw, and a lathe stands immediately to our left, just inside the door. But his most prominently positioned piece of equipment isn't anything driven by an electric motor; it is, instead, a shaving horse situated in the middle of the room beside a beautiful hickory Windsor. A drawknife sits on the horse's seat. A metal-bodied spokeshave hangs from a peg driven into the horse's frame. I notice there is no dust on the horse or the drawknife or the spokeshave.

The outside temperature is only ten degrees, and the shop is cold. I look around for a stove at which I can warm my hands. "What do you heat with?" I ask, hoping to keep the desperation from my voice.

"I got a couple of ceramic heaters." He indicates a pair of tiny black cubes, each about the size of a Kleenex box,

and I immediately regret leaving my gloves in the van.

"It'll warm up," he says. "In fact, sometimes it gets too warm in here."

Barrel-chested, wearing jeans and a bulky sweater over a flannel shirt, David looks impervious to the cold. He places a Windsor stool with bamboo turnings near the tiny heaters and seats himself. "Bring that chair over." He indicates the hickory Windsor. "Have a seat." Shivering under my coat, I obey.

David Wright grew up in Cincinnati, and after graduating from high school spent nearly ten years as an iron worker. "And then I got tired of it. I got tired of the travel, tired of working from job to job. Although the money was good, it wasn't steady. When the economy was up, there was lots of work. When the economy was down, there was none. By the time I'd come to Berea, I'd been pretty much out of work for almost a year.

"I'd always wanted to get involved in woodworking—even back in high school, and although I'd heard about Berea while I was growing up, I had no understanding of it, had never visited. Then my wife came down with some friends one summer day, and she came back home and told me all about their great wood program.

"So we came down, and I went here to Berea College for two years."

In David's shop, there is a ¾-size highboy built after a Carlyle Lynch drawing that appeared in *Fine Woodworking* fifteen years ago. I recognize the piece, having built one like it some years ago. The lower case on David's highboy, with its graceful cabriole legs, is made of walnut. Obviously, much careful work and thought went into the selection of materials and the execution of its various parts. The upper case, however, has plywood drawers with crude cutouts in place of pulls.

DAVID WRIGHT: THE VIRTUES OF SIMPLICITY

David Wright puts an edge on a tool in his shop in Berea, Kentucky.
Photographer:
Kerry Pierce

David grins when I ask him about the piece. "That was the second project I ever made. It was done here at Berea College. I attempted to do two of those. I sold the first one. This one was in a flood." He indicates a dark, water stain halfway up the sides on the upper case. "So I knocked together some plywood drawers, and I use it for storage."

Although he values the time he spent at Berea College—it was his first experience using woodworking equipment and his first experience with instruction—after two years, he transferred to Eastern Kentucky. "At that time, they had a more extensive woodworking program than Berea. So I went to Eastern Kentucky because I knew I wanted more. I wasn't sure where I wanted to go with it—outside of the fact that I wanted to get as much experience as I could.

"Eastern's program was more regimented, more academic. I took wood technology classes. I took laminating and veneering classes. While I was there, I studied everything from particleboard to drying solid lumber."

Over the last one hundred years, Berea, a small town in central Kentucky, has become a nationally known center for American craft work. In addition to a number of professional woodworkers, the town and its tourists support ceramicists, weavers and artists in stained glass. Warren May, a Berea woodworker profiled in *Woodwork* 36, estimates there are currently 35 artists' studios and shops in town. In large part, the genesis of this explosion of craft work can be traced to the many craft fairs sponsored by the college since 1900.

Too, the college has maintained a woodworking operation in which students could earn both spending money and a reduction in room-and-board expenses, an operation producing a number of high-quality reproduction pieces in the school's Wallace Nutting collection.

It was in this environment David decided to begin his career as a woodworker.

David explains: "At the time I first

came to Berea, Warren May was here and Kelly Mehler (builder of casework). Charley (Charles Harvey, *Woodwork* 34) was just getting started, working out of his house. I didn't know him at that point. Brian Boggs was getting started at that time. There was a lot going on."

Then, after almost two years at Eastern Kentucky, David decided to try making a living as a woodworker. "I had an opportunity to set up in a little shop in Charley's building. I helped him renovate the building. Then, when we had it finished, I set up shop as a chairmaker.

"I wasn't sure I wanted to make only chairs, but Charley kept encouraging me to do that. We sat down and discussed the economics of the business based on his experience. We talked about how hard it is to get started. If you go into it with the notion that you're going to make all kinds of fine furniture—beds, tables, chests—it's going to be rough going."

Like Warren May, who began as a

maker of dulcimers; and Brian Boggs, who began as a maker of post-and-rung chairs; and Charles Harvey, who began as a maker of bentwood Shaker boxes, David began his career as a professional woodworker by staking out some territory to claim as his own. "I had to face up to realities. I had no money. I had no experience. Those two factors alone are enough to put you out of business in the first year. So I focused on the Windsors." David made this decision even though he had no experience as a chairmaker, hoping that specialization would help him to achieve the same kind of name and product association enjoyed by his predecessors in Berea.

"When I opened up my chairmaking shop, I had made one chair in my life. It was a pretty ominous beginning. But I had what I needed. I had a lathe and a band saw. Then I built a bench.

"That first chair took me a month to build. I did it on my own. Charley had Michael Dunbar's book, and it gave me a place to get started. The rest I figured out on my own. Then about that time, Brian Boggs set up a seminar. This was in '88. Dave Sawyer out of Vermont came down and Curtis Buchanan was there too. We had a group of about 25 people who came in. I maybe didn't learn a lot of technical stuff, but I did get some ideas on design.

"Then I went into my shop and started making chairs. I didn't have any orders. In fact, I think it was three months before anybody came in and bought a chair. At that time, I probably had ten sitting around in my shop.

"That first order was for a set of four from these people up in Ohio. To this day, they don't know it was the first sale I ever made. I think those four chairs took me six weeks to make.

At that time, it took me almost ten days to make a chair. Now I can make a sack back in 30 hours.

David decided to leave the shop in the building owned by Charles Harvey shortly after David's wife left her job to become a full-time mother. "The overhead in that shop was about as much as the overhead here at my house. It was like I was paying for two households on a chairmaker's salary. It just didn't make sense.

"I did get some drop-in business at Charley's place (a storefront on a public street)—at least that first year, but it really fell off during the second year. I had to scramble to keep it going.

"I did some print advertising in *Ohio Antique Review* which didn't help much. So I started to do a lot of shows. I did some that were put on by the Ohio Designer Craftsmen. In fact, one year I did all three of their big shows."

Recently, David has cut back on the number of shows he does because he has found—as have so many other woodworkers—that when the costs of doing a show—transportation, lodging, meals, entry fees and lost shop time—are matched against the shows' sales potential, shows often don't make good economic sense. The most recent show he did, the Philadelphia Furniture Show, had a $1,000 booth fee, which brought the cost of doing that particular show to almost $3,000. "You've got to do quite a bit of business to make that work." He shrugs. "There's no reason for me to play the lottery; I do it every day with my work.

"Shows are hit-and-miss. Some-

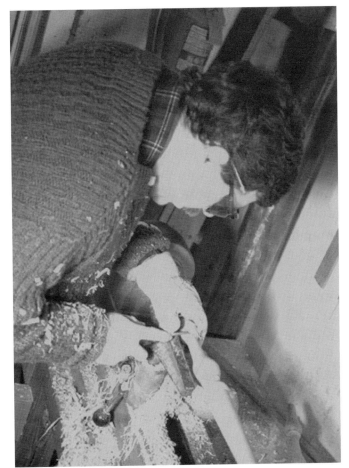

David Wright turns a baluster leg for a Windsor chair.
Photographer:
Kerry Pierce

DAVID WRIGHT: THE VIRTUES OF SIMPLICITY

A flurry of wood noodles collects at David Wright's feet as he turns a chair leg.
Photographer:
Kerry Pierce

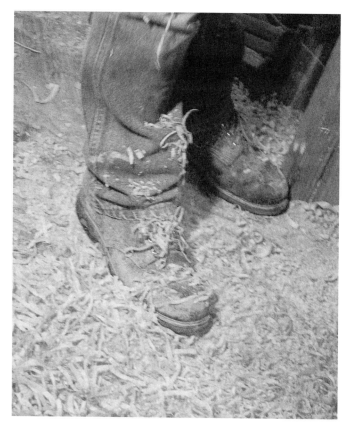

times you can do well at a small, regional show. My best ever was down here at one of the Kentucky Guild shows. I did almost $12,000 at that one show. I only had four customers, but they were the right four customers.''

Much of David's business comes from repeat customers. ''There are some who have ten, twelve, fifteen chairs. That works for me because I try to take care of my customers. I deliver good-quality chairs on time. When I get the development done on a new chair, I call them up and tell them about it. If I'm going to do a show in their area, I'll give them a call or write them a letter.''

In March of this year, David is donating a chair to be sold at an on-air auction for the benefit of the public television station in Louisville, Kentucky. ''That will give me some air time, maybe some mention in the

print press. You have to keep trying things.''

Although David sees his chairs falling into the traditional realm, none are exact copies of specific originals. ''Some are based on examples in the Wallace Nutting collection here in Berea, and I've taken some liberties with those. I think there are some things about those chairs that could have been done better, so that's what I've tried to do, although side-by-side, they'll look about the same.''

His goal artistically is to sculpt his chairs—turnings, spindles, seats and carvings—with the sharpest possible lines. ''I want my turnings to be bold so that the chair looks almost like it's alive, like it could almost walk off. That's one of the reasons why I use so much hickory. You can turn that down to a real fine diameter. Of course, with cherry, you can't go quite so far. I also shave the spindles

down farther than most chairmakers, and I carve out more wood from the seats.'' The effect of removing so much material from each part is to give his chairs, in spite of their petite size and modest splay, a very contemporary and vibrant energy.

David is also searching for ways to streamline his work methods. ''I'm not looking to hire anybody, but I want to become more production oriented. I want to better organize my own time. Like going to sawn stock.'' He lifts a sawn turning blank from his bench and holds it up. ''Look at the grain. It's just as straight as stuff I break out, but there's less labor and less waste when I use sawn material.

''And I'm trying to get ahead on bends. Last week I was in a bending frenzy because I was so excited about this oak I got.''

On a professional level, David intends to do more writing. His work has appeared in *Home Furniture*, as well as other publications. He also intends to do more teaching. In recent years, he has directed workshops at several different locations in the Kentucky area, in addition to teaching students the art and craft of chairmaking in his modest Berea shop.

''I've been on both sides of the fence work-wise. I know what it's like to be driven by somebody else. I'd rather be driven by myself. Out here in the shop, I'm doing something I love to do, something that's still a challenge. I want to improve the types of chairs I'm doing now, and I want to do new chairs. Mostly, I want every chair that I make to be better than the one that came before it.''

BEDROOM

Artist Mark Arnold
Type of object sleigh bed
Approximate size in inches $52 \times 92 \times 66$
Material cherry, cherry veneer, flexible
  plywood, bed bolts
Estimated cost of material $1,095
Estimated hours of labor 100
Price $4,500
Photographer LaJuan Spencer

> ❝ *The most satisfying aspect of my career in woodworking is the knowledge that I'm doing what I want to do, not what I have to do. Few people get to work at what they really love.*
>
> *"I feel that I'm in a career as old as mankind, an earthy craft that strives to make something useful and beautiful of an otherwise raw material."*
>
> **MARK ARNOLD, POWELL, OH**

Artist Barry Sweeney
Type of object mirror
Approximate size in inches $40 \times 22 \times 8$
Material ash, mirror
Estimated cost of material $230
Estimated hours of labor 18
Price $800
Photographer Lance Patterson

Artist Barry Sweeney
Type of object bed
Approximate size in inches $49 \times 66 \times 90$
Material cherry, mahogany, madrone burl
Estimated cost of material $800
Estimated hours of labor 120
Price $6,500
Photographer Lance Patterson

Artist Kerry Pierce
Type of object mirror
Approximate size in inches $25\frac{1}{2} \times 1\frac{1}{2} \times 14$
Material curly maple, walnut, mirror
Estimated cost of material $15
Estimated hours of labor 8
Price $200
Photographer Adam Blake

Artist Barry Sweeney
Type of object crib
Approximate size in inches $48 \times 55 \times 32$
Material walnut, bird's-eye maple
Estimated cost of material $450
Estimated hours of labor 60
Price $3,500
Photographer Lance Patterson

JEWELRY

Artist Judy Ditmer
Type of object earrings
Approximate size in inches $2 \times 1\frac{3}{8} \times \frac{3}{4}$
Material wenge, pink ivorywood
Estimated cost of material $2.50
Estimated hours of labor $\frac{1}{2}$
Price $55
Photographer Judy Ditmer

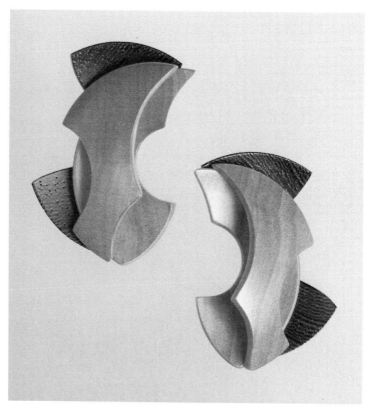

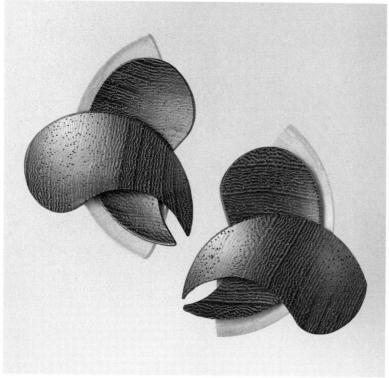

Artist Judy Ditmer
Type of object earrings
Approximate size in inches
$1\frac{3}{4} \times 1\frac{3}{4} \times \frac{5}{8}$
Material eastern hornbeam, wenge
Estimated cost of material $1.50
Estimated hours of labor $\frac{1}{2}$
Price $55
Photographer Judy Ditmer

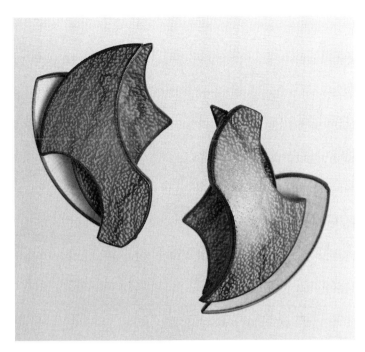

Artist Judy Ditmer
Type of object earrings
Material eastern hop hornbeam,
  marblewood
Approximate size in inches $2 \times 1\frac{1}{2} \times \frac{3}{4}$
Estimated cost of material $1.50
Estimated hours of labor $\frac{1}{2}$
Price $55
Photographer Judy Ditmer

Artist Judy Ditmer
Type of object earrings
Approximate size in inches $2 \times 1\frac{3}{4} \times \frac{5}{8}$
Material Bradford pear, wenge
Estimated cost of material $1.50
Estimated hours of labor $\frac{1}{2}$
Price $55
Photographer Judy Ditmer

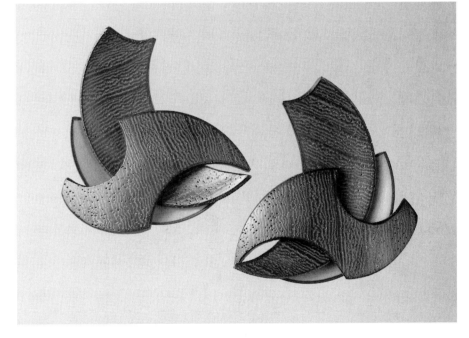

Artist Judy Ditmer

Type of object earrings

Approximate size in inches $1\frac{1}{2} \times 1\frac{1}{2} \times \frac{5}{8}$

Material wenge, Masur birch

Estimated cost of material $1.50

Estimated hours of labor $\frac{1}{2}$

Price $55

Photographer Judy Ditmer

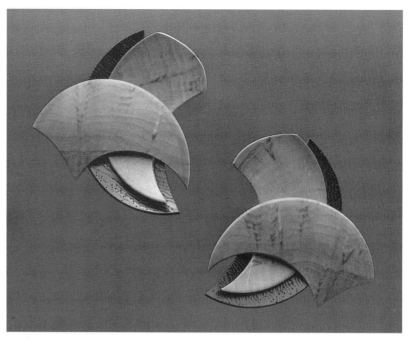

Artist Judy Ditmer

Type of object earrings

Approximate size in inches $2 \times \frac{3}{4} \times \frac{1}{4}$

Material dogwood, niobium, hornbeam,
    black onyx, brass

Estimated cost of material $3

Estimated hours of labor $\frac{1}{4}$

Price $38

Photographer Judy Ditmer

Artist Judy Ditmer
Type of object earrings
Left pair
    Approximate size in inches $1\frac{1}{2} \times \frac{5}{8} \times \frac{1}{4}$
    Material fishtail oak, rose of Sharon,
    porcelain, yellow jade
    Estimated cost of material $3
    Estimated hours of labor $\frac{1}{3}$
    Price $36
Right pair
    Approximate size in inches: $1 \times 1 \times 1\frac{1}{4}$
    Material pink ivorywood, wenge
    Estimated cost of material $1
    Estimated hours of labor $\frac{1}{4}$
    Price $28
Photographer Judy Ditmer

Artist Judy Ditmer
Type of object brooch
Left
    Approximate size in inches $1\frac{1}{4} \times 1\frac{1}{4} \times \frac{1}{4}$
    Material ebony, rose of Sharon
    Estimated cost of material $.75
    Estimated hours of labor $\frac{1}{4}$
    Price $25
Right
    Approximate size in inches $1\frac{1}{4} \times 2 \times \frac{1}{4}$
    Material eastern hop hornbeam, pink
    ivorywood, ebony
    Estimated cost of material $.75
    Estimated hours of labor $\frac{1}{4}$
    Price $20
Photographer Judy Ditmer

A TRUE ACCOUNTING OF HIDDEN COSTS BY JUDY DITMER

It still amazes me how many people who haven't tried it think it must be easy to make a living as an artisan. But it's so much more than just packing up the car and going off to the local flea market/craft show.

Retailing through shows is demanding physically and emotionally. There is an almost absurd proliferation of shows, yet it is difficult to find good ones, i.e., where you can sell enough work to make up for all the time away from the studio and the many other costs you have already incurred. Shows known to attract serious buyers also attract lots of applicants, sometimes hundreds or even thousands. Many shows invite a percentage of applicants to return unjuried, in effect reducing the number of available spaces for new applicants. This fact may not be made clear in the show's prospectus. It is entirely possible you will be one of two thousand applicants vying for 50 or 100 spaces. At those odds, a great deal of excellent work (like yours) is most certainly being turned away.

Application fees, often in the $20-$30 range, are virtually always nonrefundable. Also, more and more shows are requiring booth fees, often in the $250-500 range, to be paid with the application; such fees are nonrefundable upon acceptance. In other words, you are asked to make a substantial financial commitment to an exhibit opportunity that has not actually been offered to you in order to be considered for that opportunity. Few shows offer tenure, so you must apply again each year. You may have done well last year or for years at a stretch, but you can't know that you'll be able to do the show again next year. Thus, to be certain of filling your retail schedule, you will often need to apply to several shows for each weekend you wish to do a show. This necessitates an outlay of at least hundreds, probably thousands, of dollars before you even have any shows scheduled. Keep in mind, many of those fees are nonrefundable. Application and booth fees paid and sacrificed to keep your schedule full become part of your overhead. Whatever you do sell at the shows you attend must pay for this expense as well as the cost of goods, show overhead, travel costs, downtime after the show and so forth.

All this—simply scheduling retail shows—is thus a very complex, expensive and time-consuming proposition. The cost of the time needed for these tasks (and it does cost; even if you do not pay yourself for this time, it is no longer available to produce inventory) must be paid for by the work you sell. And this is only one of many nonproduction areas in a small craft business requiring considerable thought, attention and strategizing. Other nonproduction areas would include documenting and publicizing your work, research and development, record keeping, inventorying supplies and finished work, travel and education and so forth.

Of course, almost anyone who is at the point of contemplating earning a living by selling their work will realize they must cover their production time and the cost of the materials they use. They may also have some concept of overhead, but not many will understand just how much time and money will be spent on necessary but nonproduction aspects of building and running a business. I have observed that many craft artists—myself included—consistently underestimate the real costs of such less-visible expenditures and thus fail to include them in the price of the work.

My own Rule #1 is this: In spite of prevailing beliefs, ultimately you cannot make up for underpricing your work by selling more of it.

Artist Judy Ditmer
Type of object bowl
Approximate size in inches 3¾ × 15
Material figured maple
Estimated cost of material $30
Estimated hours of labor 3
Price $350
Photographer Judy Ditmer

> " When you're trying to judge
> the accuracy of the price
> you've put on that one-of-kind-piece,
> try this test: Imagine that someone
> comes along and says: 'Terrific! I'd
> like to have ten more of them as soon
> as you can make them.' If your heart
> falls, you've probably underpriced your
> work."
>
> **JUDY DITMER, PIQUA, OH**

STORAGE

Artist W. Richard Goehring
Type of object corner cabinet
Approximate size in inches $78 \times 18 \times 40$
Material butternut
Estimated cost of material $180
Estimated hours of labor 120
Price $2,800
Photographer W.R. Goehring

Artist Beth Ann Harrington
Type of object sideboard
Approximate size in inches $40 \times 58 \times 22$
Material white oak, various veneers, brass
Estimated cost of material $400
Estimated hours of labor 160
Price $5,200
Photographer Lance Patterson

Artist Jake
Type of object dresser
Approximate size in inches $60 \times 34 \times 22$
Material bird's-eye maple, curly maple, cherry
Estimated cost of material $600
Estimated hours of labor 45
Price $3,600
Photographer Tony Grant

Artist Jake

Type of object chest

Approximate size in inches $36 \times 20 \times 16$

Material bubinga, katalox, ebonized
mahogany

Estimated cost of material $260

Estimated hours of labor 50

Price $2,500

Photographer Tony Grant

Artist Jonathan W. McLean

Type of object breakfront

Approximate size in inches $84 \times 78 \times 22$

Material mahogany, satinwood, tulipwood,
ebony, holly, glass, brasses

Estimated cost of material $770

Estimated hours of labor 450

Price $16,000

Photographer Lance Patterson

Artist Gregory K. Williams
Type of object collector's cabinet
Approximate size in inches $50 \times 18 \times 14$
Material curly maple, cherry
Estimated cost of material $100
Estimated hours of labor 40
Price $1,200
Photographer Jerry Anthony

Artist Randy Bemont
Type of object home office
Approximate size in inches $84 \times 84 \times 24$
Materials cherry and cherry MDF, Shaker knobs
Estimated cost of material $1,000
Estimated hours of labor 90
Price $2,900
Photographer Randy Bemont

Artist Mark Arnold

Type of object wardrobe

Approximate size in inches $64 \times 20 \times 42$

Material cherry, cherry plywood, brass
hinges

Estimated cost of material $700

Estimated hours of labor 72

Price $3,200

Photographer Mike Sleeper

Artist Mark Arnold

Type of object highboy

Approximate size in inches $70 \times 18\frac{1}{2} \times 39$

Material cherry, poplar, madrone burl

Estimated cost of material $700

Estimated hours of labor 225

Price $8,600

Photographer Lance Patterson

> *You must turn out a product that is of high quality and craftsmanship, along with being something the public wants and is willing to pay for."*
>
> **TIM DETWEILER, GERMANTOWN, OH**

Artist Mark Arnold
Type of object entertainment center
Approximate size in inches $82 \times 24 \times 108$
Material cherry, cherry plywood,
   Eurohinges, Shaker knobs
Estimated cost of material $1,000
Estimated hours of labor 110
Price $4,850
Photographer Mike Sleeper

Artist Kerry Pierce
Type of object magazine stand
Approximate size in inches $40 \times 12 \times 11\frac{3}{16}$
Material white oak, walnut
Estimated cost of material $50
Estimated hours of labor 12
Price $300
Photographer Adam Blake

WOODEN WARE

Artist Mark Parish
Type of object vase
Approximate size in inches 10½×6
Material black ebony
Estimated cost of material $380
Estimated hours of labor 23
Price $2,800
Photographer Celuch Creative

Artist Mark Parish
Type of object vase
Approximate size in inches 8×6
Material white elm
Estimated cost of material $100
Estimated hours of labor 16
Price $1,400
Photographer Celuch Creative

Artist Mark Parish
Type of object vase
Approximate size in inches 11×7
Material cocobolo, rosewood
Estimated cost of material $190
Estimated hours of labor 16
Price $530
Photographer Celuch Creative

Artist Gregory K. Williams
Type of object lamp
Approximate size in inches 18×6×6
Material cherry, walnut
Estimated cost of material $20
Estimated hours of labor 6
Price $150
Photographer Jerry Anthony

Artist Kerry Vesper
Type of object bowl
Approximate size in inches 8½×17×14
Material African padauk, Baltic birch
Estimated cost of material $35
Estimated hours of labor 40
Price $1,200
Photographer Jeff Noble

Artist Kerry Vesper
Type of object bowl
Approximate size in inches $8 \times 7 \times 8$
Material cocobolo, Baltic birch
Estimated cost of material $25
Estimated hours of labor 5
Price $300
Photographer Jeff Noble

Artist Mark Parish
Type of object vase
Approximate size in inches $9\frac{1}{2} \times 6$
Material zebrawood
Estimated cost of material $140
Estimated hours of labor 18
Price $470
Photographer Celuch Creative

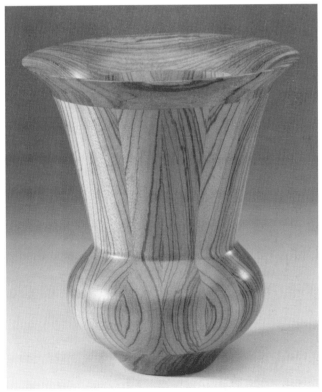

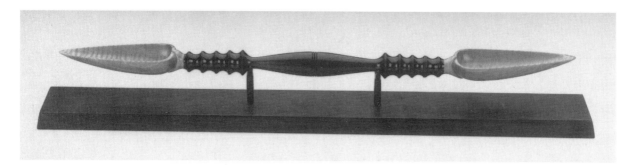

Artist Norm Sartorius
Type of object double spoon
Approximate size in inches 1¼ × 2 × 18
Material Madagascar rosewood, curly pink
  ivorywood

Estimated cost of material $15
Estimated hours of labor 30
Price $1,500
Photographer Jim Osborn

Artist Norm Sartorius
Type of object spoon
Approximate size in inches 1 × 14 × 4
Material ebony, bird's-eye maple

Estimated cost of material $2
Estimated hours of labor 15
Price $600
Photographer Jim Osborn

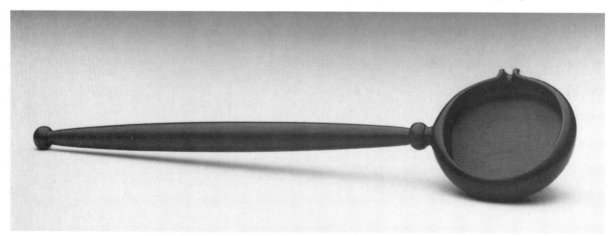

Artist Norm Sartorius
Type of object spouted spoon
Approximate size in inches 1 × 14 × 4
Material bloodwood

Estimated cost of material $5
Estimated hours of labor 20
Price $500
Photographer Jim Osborn

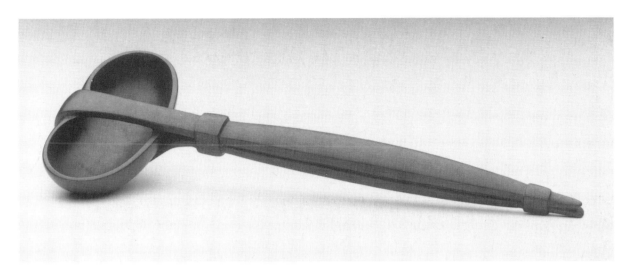

Artist Norm Sartorius
Type of object spoon
Approximate size in inches $1\frac{1}{2} \times 10 \times 3$
Material imbuya

Estimated cost of material $2
Estimated hours of labor 20
Price $800
Photographer Jim Osborn

Artist Stanley and Susan Jennings
Type of object flatware serving set
  for eight
Approximate size in inches $5 \times 24 \times 20$
Material cherry, curly maple
Estimated cost of material $10
Estimated hours of labor 20+
Price $500
Photographer Susan Jennings

Artist Stanley and Susan Jennings
Type of object measuring cup set
Approximate size in inches $3 \times 15 \times 24$
Material spalted maple
Estimated cost of material $8
Estimated hours of labor 8
Price $200
Photographer Susan Jennings

Artist Beth Ann Harrington
Type of object doorbell cover
Approximate size in inches $11 \times 8\frac{1}{2} \times 2$
Material white oak, various veneers
Estimated cost of material $25
Estimated hours of labor 10
Price $350
Photographer Lance Patterson

Artist Tom Douglass
Type of object pipe box
Approximate size in inches $22 \times 4\frac{1}{2} \times 5\frac{1}{2}$
Material tulip poplar
Estimated cost of material $20
Estimated hours of labor 50+
Price $1,100
Photographer Tom Douglass

Artist Tom Douglass
Type of object spoon board
Approximate size in inches $18 \times 6\frac{1}{2}$
Material tulip poplar
Estimated cost of material $10
Estimated hours of labor 40+
Price $900
Photographer Tom Douglass

Artist Judy Ditmer
Type of object lidded box
Approximate size in inches 3½ × 2¾
Material unknown
Estimated cost of material $5
Estimated hours of labor ¾
Price $55
Photographer Judy Ditmer

Artist Judy Ditmer
Type of object egg boxes
Approximate size in inches ⅝ × ½
Material assorted woods
Estimated cost of material (each) $.50
Estimated hours of labor (each) ⅕
Price (each) $12
Photographer Judy Ditmer

Artist Judy Ditmer
Type of object birdhouse ornaments
Approximate size in inches $2 \times 1\frac{1}{2}$
Material assorted woods, brass peg, ribbon
Estimated cost of material (each) $2.50
Estimated hours of labor (each) $\frac{1}{3}$
Price (each) $25
Photographer Judy Ditmer

Artist Judy Ditmer
Type of object finger tops
Approximate size in inches $1\frac{1}{2} \times 1\frac{1}{2}$
Material assorted woods
Estimated cost of material $.03
Estimated hours of labor $\frac{1}{4}$
Price $3
Photographer Judy Ditmer

Artist Judy Ditmer
Type of object bowl
Approximate size in inches 3½ × 8
Material figured maple
Estimated cost of material $20
Estimated hours of labor 2
Price $175
Photographer Judy Ditmer

> *Production work is my bread and butter, so it is very important for me to price it properly so that it will sell and so that I make enough money on it. I figure the smaller and less expensive an item is, the better I should do with it, that is, I should go over my 'target rate' on, say, spinning tops. These wholesale for $1.50, and I make thousands of them every year, most of which are sold at that wholesale price. If I am not going to make any money on them, I am going to resent every damn one of them. Instead, because I sell them at a high enough price to make money on them, I think as I make them: 'What a great day job this is! It's even helping me to keep in practice and pay for the equipment.'*

JUDY DITMER, PIQUA, OH

Artist Judy Ditmer
Type of object bowl
Approximate size in inches 3 × 10
Material cherry
Estimated cost of material $20
Estimated hours of labor 3½
Price $200
Photographer Judy Ditmer

Artist Judy Ditmer
Type of object bowl
Approximate size in inches 4½×12½
Material cherry
Estimated cost of material $25
Estimated hours of labor 2½
Price $300
Photographer Judy Ditmer

Artist Judy Ditmer
Type of object bowl
Approximate size in inches 5½×14
Material cherry
Estimated cost of material $35
Estimated hours of labor 3
Price $350
Photographer Judy Ditmer

Artist Judy Ditmer
Type of object bowl
Approximate size in inches 6×7
Material figured maple
Estimated cost of material $30
Estimated hours of labor 2½
Price $300
Photographer Judy Ditmer

Artist Judy Ditmer
Type of object bowl
Approximate size in inches $4½ \times 9$
Material apple
Estimated cost of material $25
Estimated hours of labor 2½
Price $275
Photographer Judy Ditmer

Judy Ditmer's Figured Maple Bowl

Judy, herself, harvests many of her bowl-turning blanks. She cut the blank from which this particular bowl was turned from a fallen tree in a cemetery near her home in Piqua, Ohio.

Although she is confident she can apply fair prices to her turned jewelry, she finds the pricing of bowls to be more difficult. There are several reasons for this. First, the labor is not concentrated in a single turning and finishing session. It is, instead, spread out over a period of months during which the blank is harvested, seasoned, rough turned, seasoned again, then finish turned. This makes it hard to keep accurate records of the time required for an individual bowl. Second, Judy points to another, more subtle difficulty: The price of every successful bowl "has to account for the time spent making bowls that didn't work out." Every bowl she turns is unique, and unfortunately not all convey the sense of aesthetic completeness she expects to see in her finished work. Substandard bowls must be discarded. Last, there is the issue of market size. While her jewelry appeals to many of the women who visit her booth at craft shows, a much smaller percentage of the people who see her work are interested in purchasing bowls. This means she can't price the bowls to move. She must in-stead set prices, then find the patience to allow the bowls to sell at those prices.

In spite of these problems, she cites a strong reason to continue making larger turned objects, like her bowls: She has found that the presence of bowls in her portfolio enhances her chances of getting into certain retail shows. "This is more of that bigger-is-better thinking," she explains.

Artist Judy Ditmer
Type of object bowl
Approximate size in inches 3¾ × 15
Material figured maple
Estimated cost of material $30
Estimated hours of labor 3
Price $350
Photographer Judy Ditmer

Artist Tim Detweiler
Type of object working combination lock
Approximate size in inches $16 \times 10 \times 4$
Material cherry, walnut
Estimated cost of material $40
Estimated hours of labor 30
Price $800
Photographer Tim Detweiler

Artist Tim Detweiler
Type of object working padlock
Approximate size in inches $8 \times 4\frac{1}{2} \times 2\frac{1}{4}$
Material many woods
Estimated cost of material $4.50
Estimated hours of labor $2\frac{1}{2}$
Price $60
Photographer Tim Detweiler

" *Most of my production work is actually one-of-a-kind. I work hard for that because it not only adds to the quality and perceived value of the work to the purchaser, it also helps to keep me from getting bored with the work. In addition, it makes proper use of one of the most exciting aspects of the nature of lathe work: that one may be designing and making the piece at the same time. But here I am speaking of very high-end kind of pieces, the kind that have a lot of thinking time involved, which is separate from at least much of the making time. These are pieces that may require working out new processes, becoming familiar with new materials, and experimenting with both. Such pieces are more difficult to price, partly because the prices will be orders of magnitude higher than production work, but also because prevailing prices for what is perceived as comparable work in the marketplace will become more important. Another factor is that the results of your work may be less predictable at the higher end: Piece A may take you hours of miserable, sweaty concentration, but for whatever reason, just wasn't successful. But when you made Piece B, you were in that rare state of grace to which we all aspire—you felt good, the wood felt good, it was all just happening—and the piece came out fantastic in just half the time it often takes.*

"Well, you're just not going to be able to get a fair price for that first piece so the price of the whiz-bang piece had better reflect that reality. In effect, the making of that first piece is part of the cost of making that successful second piece. *That's because we are not machines; we are artists. If we could know, absolutely, every time we put a gouge to the wood what the result would be, then it would never have that astonishing, unexpected, surprising* magic *it sometimes does when that undefinable something is happening.*

"On a practical level, you need to remember that when you price things."

JUDY DITMER, PIQUA, OH

LIST OF CONTRIBUTORS

Mark Arnold

189-A W. Olentangy Street

Powell OH 43065

(614) 792-5545

Randy Bemont

11 Pine Hill Drive

Granby CT 06035-2817

(860) 653-0316

Curtis Buchanan

208 E. Main Street

Jonesborough TN 37659

(423) 753-5160

Sal Cretella

54 Clover Road

Bristol CT 06010

(860) 582-8724

Tim Detweiler

6979 S. Diamond Mill Road

Germantown OH 45327

(937) 855-3838

Judy Ditmer

502 E. Greene Street

Piqua OH 45356-2420

(937) 773-1116

Tom Douglass

RD #1, Box 38

Hopwood PA 15445

(724) 438-4203

Mike Dunbar

44 Timber Swamp Road

Hampton NH 03842

(603) 929-9801

Jim Fiola

2 East Trail

Branchville NJ 07826

(973) 948-3260

W. Richard Goehring

P.O. Box 586

Gambier OH 43022

(740) 392-0427

Joe Graham

1192 Webster Road

Jefferson OH 44047

(440) 576-0311

Beth Ann Harrington

116 Park Street

Ithaca NY 14850

(781) 395-2750

John Hartcorn

100 Kilsyth Road

Brighton MA 02135

(781) 396-5330

Jake

12711 East Street

Boulder CA 95006

(408) 338-1905

Stanley and Susan Jennings

Route 1, Box 62

Thornton WV 26440

(304) 892-3270

Chris Kamm

3871 E. Sweeten Creek Road

Arden NC 28704

(828) 681-0043

glarnerdes@aol.com

Brent Karner

322 Rt. 100 N.

Ludlow VT 05149

(802) 228-8395

Po Shun Leong

8546 Oso Avenue

Winnetka CA 91306-1341

(818) 341-1559

Jonathan W. McLean

763 Waverly Street

Framingham MA 01702

(508) 626-7675

Barry Middleton

3530 Carmen Road

Schenectady NY 12303

(518) 357-4737

Mark Parish

5636 Green Ridge Road SE

New Philadelphia OH 44663

(330) 343-6357

Kerry Pierce

3104 Mudhouse

Lancaster OH 43130

(740) 653-7424

knp@netpluscom.com

Owen Rein

P.O. Box 1162

Mountain View AK 72560

(870) 269-5381

Richard Rothbard

P.O. Box 480

Slate Hill NY 10973

(914) 355-2400

Norm Sartorius

1807 Plum Street

Parkersburg WV 26101

(304) 485-3394

Barry Sweeney

1 Joseph Pace Road

Medfield MA 02052

(508) 359-8040

bsweeney@aol.com

Kerry Vesper

116 E. Ellis Drive

Tempe AZ 85282

(602) 962-4801

FAX (602) 962-4801

kerryves@phnx.uswest.net

Gregory K. Williams

Zeke Towne Woodworks

1865 Celina Road

Burkesville KY 42117

(502) 433-7400

David Wright

P.O. Box 132

Berea KY 40403

(606) 986-7962

SOURCES OF SUPPLY

Constantine's

2050 Eastchester Road

Bronx NY 10461

(800) 223-8087

Garrett Wade

161 Avenue of the Americas

New York NY 10013

(800) 221-2942

Grizzly Imports, Inc.

2406 Reach Road

Williamsport PA 17701

(800) 523-4777

Hartville Tool

940 W. Maple Street

Hartville OH 44632

(800) 345-2396

Klingspor's Sanding Catalogue

P.O. Box 3737

Hickory NC 28603-3737

(800) 228-0000

Lee Valley Tools, Ltd.

P.O. Box 1780

Ogdensburg NY 13669-0490

(800) 871-8158

McFeely's

1620 Wythe Road

P.O. Box 11169

Lynchburg VA 24506-1169

Meisel Hardware Specialties

P.O. Box 70

Mound MN 55364-0070

(800) 441-9870

Sears Power and Hand Tools

20 Presidential Drive

Roselle IL 60172

(800) 377-7414

Tool Crib of the North

P.O. Box 14040

Grand Forks ND 58208-4040

(800) 358-3096

Trend-lines

135 American Legion Way

Revere MA 02151

(800) 767-9999

Wood Carvers Supply, Inc.

P.O. Box 7500

Englewood FL 34295-7500

(800) 284-6229

Woodcraft

210 Wood County Industrial Park

P.O. Box 1686

Parkersburg WV 26102-1686

(800) 225-1153

Woodhaven

5323 Kimberly Road

Davenport IA 52806-7126

(800) 344-6657

Woodpeckers, Inc.

P.O. Box 29510

Parma OH 44129

(800) 752-0725

Woodworker's Hardware

P.O. Box 180

Sauk Rapids MN 56379

(800) 383-0130

Woodworker's Supply

1108 North Glenn Road

Casper WY 82601

(800) 645-9292

INDEX

MORE GREAT BOOKS FOR PROFITABLE WOODWORKING!

Make Your Woodworking Pay for Itself, Revised Edition—Find simple hints for selling your work to generate extra income! You'll find hints on easy ways to save on wood and tools, ideas for projects to sell, guidance for handling money and more! Plus, new information on home-business zoning and tax facts keeps you up-to-date. #70320/$18.99/128 pages/20 b&w illus./paperback

How to Make $40,000 a Year With Your Woodworking—This guide takes the guesswork out of starting and running your own woodworking enterprise. It provides a solid business program using charts, forms and graphs that illustrate how to define objectives, create a realistic plan, market your work, manage your staff and keep good, accurate records with formulas for projecting overhead, labor costs, profit margins, taxes and more. #70405/$19.99/128 pages/30 b&w illus./paperback

Small-Production Woodworking for the Home Shop—Whether fulfilling client orders or making holiday gifts, you'll learn the best ways to "set up shop" in your home for production runs that save time and money. Professional woodworkers share their proven techniques for manufacturing pieces in all shapes, sizes and complexities. #70385/$23.99/128 pages/180 b&w illus./paperback

Earn a Second Income From Your Woodworking—This is the book you've been looking for! It provides you with all the inspiration and how-to information you need to make your dream a reality with the help of 15 profiles of successful woodworkers. Each one is jammed with tips, tricks and techniques. #70377/$22.99/128 pages/42 b&w illustrations/paperback

Woodworker's Guide to Pricing Your Work—Turn your hobby into profit! You'll find out how other woodworkers set their prices and sell their products. You'll learn how to estimate average materials cost per project, increase your income without sacrificing quality or enjoyment, build repeat and referral business, manage a budget and much more! #70268/$18.99/160 pages/paperback

Woodworker's Guide to Selecting and Milling Wood—Save money on lumber as you preserve the great tradition of felling, milling and drying your own wood. Loads of full-color illustrations will help you identify the right wood for every job. #70248/$22.99/144 pages/128 b&w illus., 32 color photos

Good Wood Handbook, Second Edition—Now in paperback! This handy reference gives you all the information you need to select and use the right wood for the job—before you buy. You'll discover valuable information on a wide selection of commercial softwoods and hardwoods—from common uses, color and grain to how the wood glues and takes finish. #70451/$14.99/128 pages/250 color illus./paperback

The Woodworker's Source Book, Second Edition—Shop for woodworking supplies from home! This book includes compiled listings for everything from books and videos to plans and associations. Each listing has an address and telephone number and is rated in terms of quality and price. #70281/$19.99/160 pages/50 illus.

Smart Shelving & Storage Solutions—These innovative and inexpensive storage solutions are perfect for do-it-yourselfers. From book shelves, chests and cabinets to armoires, closet systems and benches, you'll find more than 27 woodworking projects to help you make the most of your space—whether it's under the bed, over the sink or in the garage. #70445/$24.99/144 pages/360 color, 40 b&w illus./paperback

The Weekend Woodworker—A fantastic resource for the straightforward, step-by-step projects you like! This book offers you a range of attractive challenges, from smaller items—such as a stylish CD rack, mailbox or birdhouse—to larger, easy-to-assemble projects including a wall cupboard, child's bed, computer workstation and coffee table. Each project provides clear and easy step-by-step instructions, photographs and diagrams, ideal for both the beginner and expert. #70456/$22.99/144 pages/200 color photos/paperback

How to Design and Build Your Ideal Woodshop—Designed especially for the home-shop woodworker, this guide features dozens of practical alternatives, tips and solutions for transforming attics, garages, basements or out-buildings into efficient and safe woodshops. Clear instructions also include photos, drawings and considerations for electricity, lighting, ventilation, plumbing, accessibility, insulation, flooring and more. #70397/$24.99/160 pages/paperback

Building Classic Antique Furniture With Pine—This book offers a range of affordable and user-friendly furniture projects, including antique-style tables, desks, cabinets, boxes, chests and more. Each step-by-step project includes numbered steps with photos and drawings, material lists, a brief description of the function and history of each piece as well as the estimated current market value of both the original piece and the reproduction. #70396/$22.99/144 pages/216 color illus./paperback

How to Build Classic Garden Furniture—This easy, step-by-step guide will have you anxious to begin crafting this elegant outdoor furniture. The 20 projects are designed to withstand years of outdoor exposure with minimal care, and are versatile enough to compliment any home's style. Each beautiful piece is made easy to accomplish with full-color illustrations, numbered steps, close-up photos and alternatives for design, wood selection and finishing. #70395/$24.99/128 pages/275 color, 69 b&w illus./paperback

Beautiful Wooden Gifts You Can Make in a Weekend—This fun and unique book offers you 20 different gift projects that can be built in a couple of days, including step-by-step instructions for jewelry boxes, toys, kitchen accessories, puzzle boxes and more. An easy-to-follow format includes line drawings, photos, illustrations and complete tools and materials lists. #70384/$22.99/128 pages/20 color, 160 b&w illus./paperback

The Woodworker's Guide to Shop Math—This hands-on guide takes mathematical principles from the chalkboard to the wood shop, using real-life shop situations to make math easy and practical. Also provided is an overview of basic arithmetic, a review of common units of measurement, and several conversion charts and tables for fractions, multiplication, weights, decimals, volume, area, temperature and more. #70406/$22.99/208 pages/169 b&w illus./paperback

Making Elegant Gifts From Wood—Develop your woodworking skills and make over 30 gift-quality projects at the same time. You'll find everything you're looking to create in your gifts—variety, timeless styles, pleasing proportions and imaginative designs that call for the best woods. Plus, technique sidebars and hardware installation tips make your job even easier. *#70331/$24.99/128 pages/30 color, 120 b&w illus.*

Making Wooden Mechanical Models—Discover plans for 15 handsome and incredibly clever machines with visible wheels, cranks, pistons and other moving parts made of wood. Expertly photographed and complete with materials lists and diagrams, the plans call for a challenging variety of techniques and procedures. *#70288/$21.99/144 pages/341 illus./ paperback*

Making More Wooden Mechanical Models—Turn the cranks, press the buttons and pull the levers on 15 projects that make great gifts. Despite their seemingly elaborate configurations, they're simple to make following this guide's complete step-by-step instructions. You'll find that every project features a full-color close up of the finished piece, in addition to hand-rendered drawings, cutting lists and special tips for making difficult steps easier. *#70444/$24.99/128 pages/15 color, 250 b&w illus./paperback*

Creating Beautiful Boxes With Inlay Techniques—Now building elegant boxes is easy with this handy reference featuring 13 full-color, step-by-step projects! Thorough directions and precise drawings will have you creating beautiful inlaid boxes with features ranging from handcut dovetails to hidden compartments. *#70368/$24.99/128 pages/230 color, 30 b&w illus./paperback*

Tune Up Your Tools—Bring your tools back to perfect working order and experience safe, accurate cutting, drilling and sanding. With this handy reference you'll discover how to tune up popular woodworking machines, instruction for aligning your tools, troubleshooting charts and many other tips. *#70308/$22.99/144 pages/150 b&w illus./ paperback*

Display Cabinets You Can Customize—Go beyond building to designing furniture. You'll receive step-by-step instructions to the base projects—the starting points for a wide variety of pieces, such as display cabinets, tables and cases. Then you'll learn about customizing techniques. You'll see how to adapt a glass-front cabinet; put a profile on a cabinet by using molding; get a different look by using stained glass or changing the legs and much more! *#70282/$18.99/128 pages/150 b&w illus./ paperback*

The Stanley Book of Woodworking Tools, Techniques and Projects—Become a better woodworker by mastering the fundamentals of choosing the right wood, cutting tight-fitting joints, properly using a marking gauge and much more. *#70264/$19.99/160 pages/400 color illus./ paperback*

Marvelous Wooden Boxes You Can Make—Master woodworker Jeff Greef offers plans for 20 beautiful, functional boxes, complete with drawings, cutting lists, numbered step-by-step instructions and color photographs. *#70287/$24.99/144 pages/67 color, 225 b&w illus.*

Measure Twice, Cut Once, Revised Edition—Miscalculation will be a thing of the past when you learn these effective techniques for checking and adjusting measuring tools, laying out complex measurements, fixing mistakes, making templates and much more! *#70330/$22.99/144 pages/144 color illus./paperback*

100 Keys to Woodshop Safety—Make your shop safer than ever with this manual designed to help you avoid potential pitfalls. Tips and illustrations demonstrate the basics of safe shop work—from using electricity safely and avoiding trouble with hand and power tools to ridding your shop of dangerous debris and handling finishing materials. *#70333/$17.99/64 pages/125 color illus.*